EXCESS OF BEING
LERA AUERBACH

APHORISMS

Arch Street Press
Philadelphia

EST. 2010
ARCH ST. PRESS

Arch Street Press
Philadelphia, PA • USA

Copyright © 2015 Lera Auerbach

All rights reserved, including the right to reproduce this book or portions thereof in any form whatsoever. For information on reproducing or licensing rights, please contact Arch Street Press: contact@archstreetpress.org.

First Arch Street Press edition January 2015

ARCH STREET PRESS, ARCH ST. PRESS
and colophon are registered trademarks of Arch Street Press.

For information about special discounts for bulk purchases, please contact Arch Street Press: sales@archstreetpress.org.

The Arch Street Press Speakers Bureau can bring authors to your live event. For more information or to book an event, visit our website at www.archstreetpress.org.

All artworks copyright © 2014 Lera Auerbach
Cover and design by Lera Auerbach

Printed in South Korea

Library of Congress Cataloging-in-Publication Data is available.

ISBN 978-1-938798-06-1
ISBN 978-1-938798-07-8 (e-book)

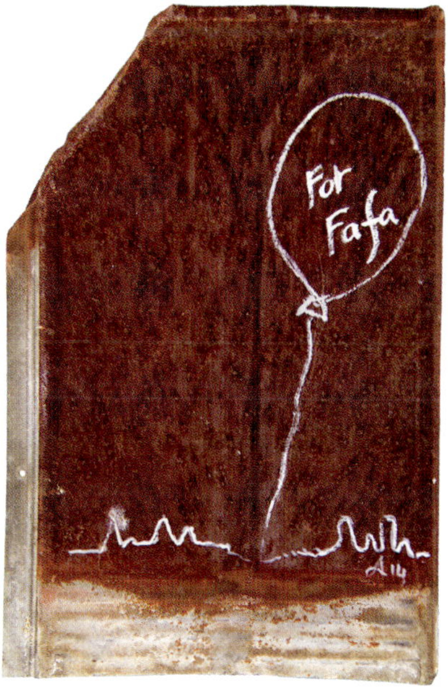
For
Fafa

ACKNOWLEDGMENTS

The author would like to thank The Best American Poetry blog where some of these aphorisms and musings first appeared; and the following friends and colleagues in random order: Robert Rimm, David Lehman, Marilyn Nelson, Josh Barkan, Waris Ahluwalia, Thomas McCarthy, John Matthias, Irene Dische, Sandy Climan, Laurie Anderson, Serge Sorokko, Tzimon Barto, John Neumeier, Jeffrey Hatcher, Vadim Gluzman, Evgeny Kissin, Dmitry Gutov, Alisa Weilerstein, Dmitry Sitkovetsky, Patricia and Chris Caswell, Rick Walker, Stacey Hardwood, Jane Gardner, Sally Barnett, Fred vonAppen, Alan Bloch, Nancy Berman, Bruce Rodgers, Antonina W. and Jean-Claude Bouis, Elisabeth and Gil Waters, Ina Schnell, Arthur Ancowitz, Jeffrey Soros, Daisy Soros, Kim Kashkashian, Elisabeth Johnson, Taylor Davis-Van Atta, James Kuslan, Robin Radin, Hans-Ulrich Duffek, Herbert and Beverly Gelfand, Séverine and Ivan Cohen, Joseph Correia, Catherine de Marignac, Sonia Simmenauer, Roswitha Wooley and Regina Fidelgolz for their invaluable support and advice; Rafael, Stella and my parents for their patience and encouragement; my dog Finek, cat Begemot and ferret Shosta for their quiet wisdom and perspective.

EXCESS OF BEING

I. Musings 11
   on music, muses and misgivings
II. Marginals 61
   on writing, readership and art
III. Findings 141
   on life and other illusions
IV. Fragile Solitudes 247
   on wings and vanishing maps of memories
V. Accidentals 281
   on relationships and other misunderstandings
VI. Eterniday 337
   on angels, demons and wannabes
VII. Trouble Clef 435
   88 keys for silent piano
VIII. Coda 455
   self-portrait

> *"Excess of being*
> *wells up in my heart…"*
>   – R.M. Rilke

musings

on music, muses and misgivings

◉

What can be better than an aphorism? Its absence.

◉

Hearing voices is not insanity,
writing them down – is.

◉

Invisibility
leaves
traces.

14   Excess of Being

A composer does not own his sounds;
the sounds own him.

I do not have performance anxiety –
I have non-performance anxiety.

I love
what I do,
but it's not mutual.

Not only sounds,
but silences
have different
colors.

Shhh… I'm cataloging silences.

An artist's
entrance
to eternity
requires a fee
in disappointment.

Musings 17

18 Excess of Being

◎

My diagnosis:
an overactive
syncopation syndrome.

◎

I *only*
have perfect pitch.
The rest is imperfect.

◎

Rehearsal: Re-hear-sal.
To rehearse is to hear
again and again,
hear it differently,
hear it anew.
Practicing is the art
of listening.

20 Excess of Being

Just remember— anything with strings attached sooner or later will make sound.

If you have a flaw – make it part of your legacy.

A living composer is a nuisance. Dead composers are much more agreeable and they don't ask for comps.

My friend T., a singer, was working very hard at establishing just the right amount of bitchiness, which she believed was essential to be taken seriously as an opera diva. I asked what constitutes the right amount of bitchiness, but the answer was too complex with too many variables for me to grasp. I guess this is why my prospects of becoming an opera diva are nil.

❊

Dress rehearsal: Playground for disasters.
World premiere: High-voltage nerves, some accidents, but great energy and memorable performance.
Second performance: No accidents, no energy – a flop.
Third performance: The real premiere.

❊

I started playing piano before I learned which was my right hand and which the left. To remember my hands correctly, I would associate the right hand with the high notes of the keyboard and the left hand with the bass notes. Even now, the words "right" and "left" remain subconsciously orchestrated. When I hear "extreme right," I can't help but imagine all these politicians speaking with high-tweeting Chip-and-Dale voices while the leftists are the slow-slurring basses, regardless of their gender or physical constitution. As a result, I can't take either side seriously.

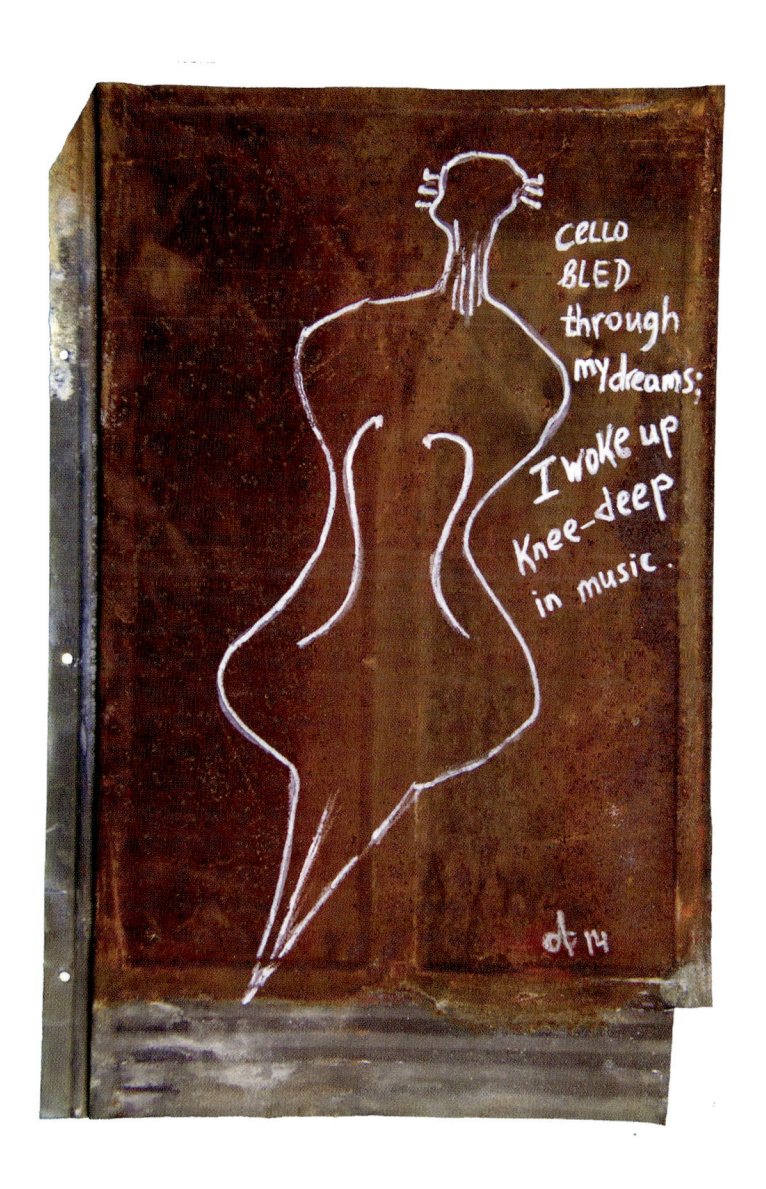

Cello bled through my dreams; I woke up knee-deep in music.

Music harmony: Not all notes are born equal.

My right and left hands don't like each other, yet both have to collaborate and share the same piano keyboard. Musical diplomacy.

When I arrived in New York for the first time, I asked H. how many composers lived in the city. H. theatrically pointed around at the skyscrapers, "Do you see all these buildings? Do you see all these windows? Behind each window, there is a composer!"
I was impressed.

Recording session:
"1st take, 2nd take, 3rd take…"
Why is it always takes and not gives? Aren't we giving it all?
"1st give, 2nd give, 3rd give."
No, you can't keep counting what you give.
Let's go back to the takes.

Certainty and good sound both reside in a soft belly.
Your guts come from your guts.

Throughout the dinner, composer X convincingly displayed his complete lack of interest in me. I even started to suspect that it was genuine.

◉

I speak
in major keys
with others
while keeping
the minor
to myself.

◉

My fees are too high? But you are not paying for my work;
I work for free. My fees are for all the time I'll spend
procrastinating.

◉

Job description: putting black dots on five horizontal lines.
The strangest thing is – I'm making a living doing that.

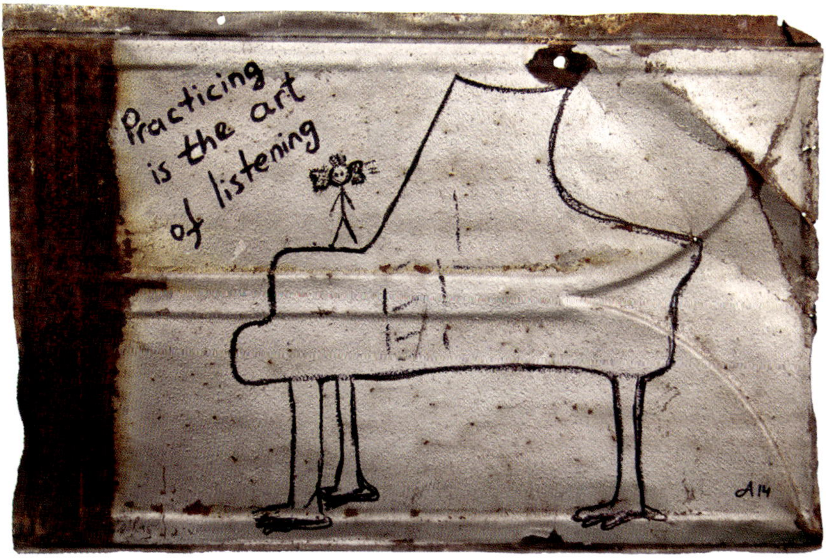
Practicing
is the art
of listening
A14

Inspiration may come from the Muse,
but insecurity is all my own.

I prefer writing to practicing piano.
Writing can be done in bed.

Cello
bled
through my dreams;
I woke up
knee-deep
in music.

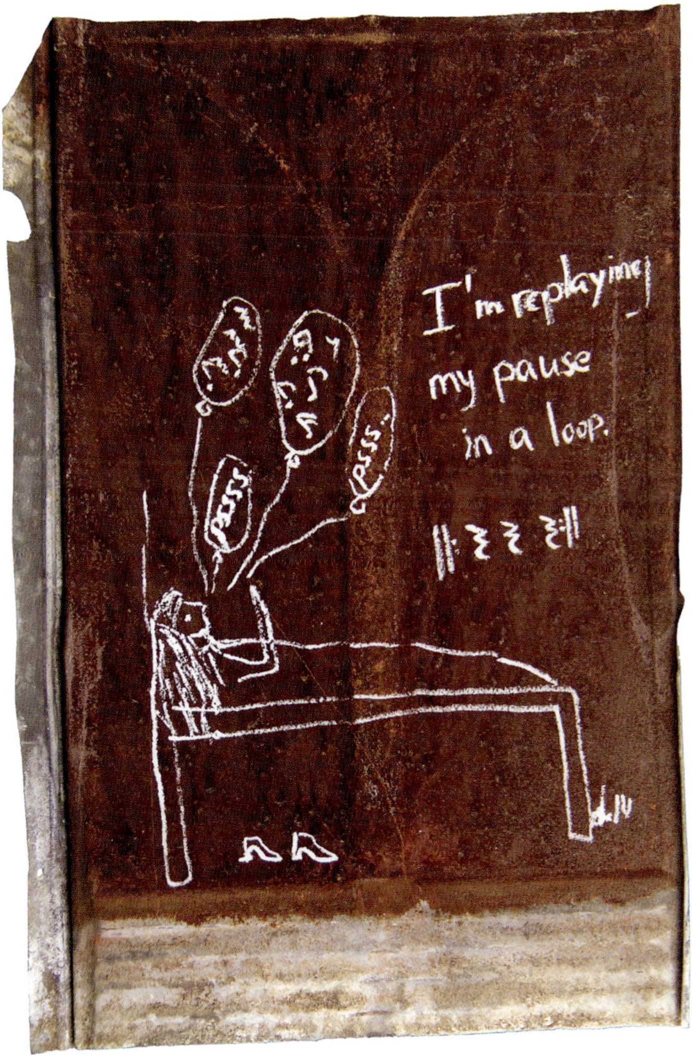
I'm replaying
my pause
in a loop.

◉

If you are worried about spoiling the freshness of your interpretation by too much practicing, it means that your interpretation was rotten from the start.

◉

My notes misbehave.

◉

Sometimes I feel tempted
to screw up badly –
just to see what happens.

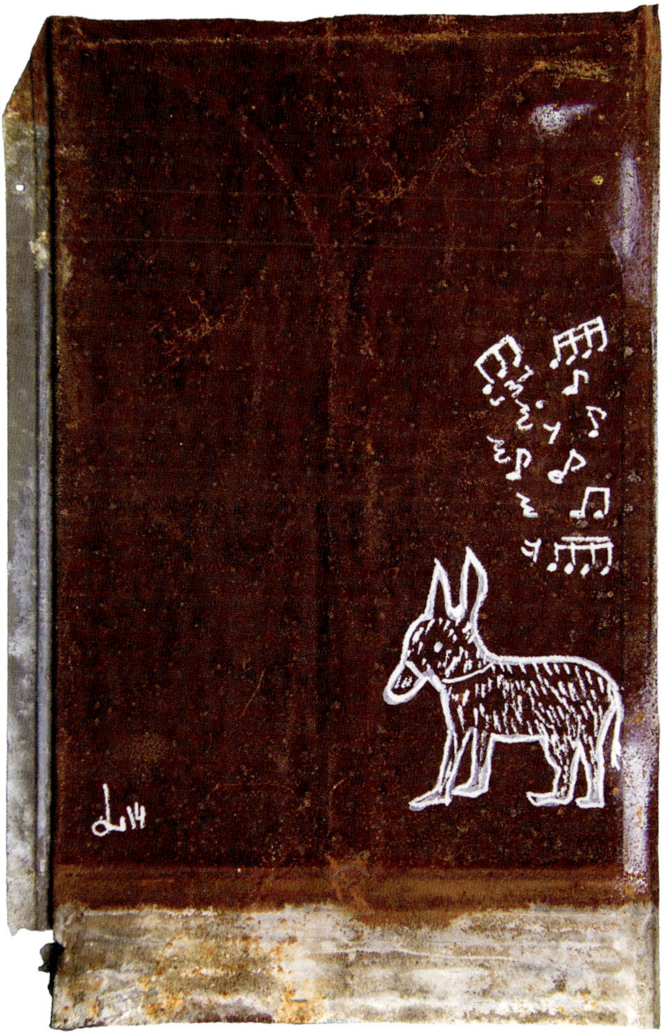

32 Excess of Being

> There are only two types of composers: composing composers and decomposing composers.
>
> Adagio
>
> A 14

❂

Troubled clef
of treble hopes
trembling
from the touch
of despairing tremolo.

❂

The pauses
in Chopin's mazurkas
burn the air.

❂

Classical musicians
are vultures –
they feed on the dead.

34 Excess of Being

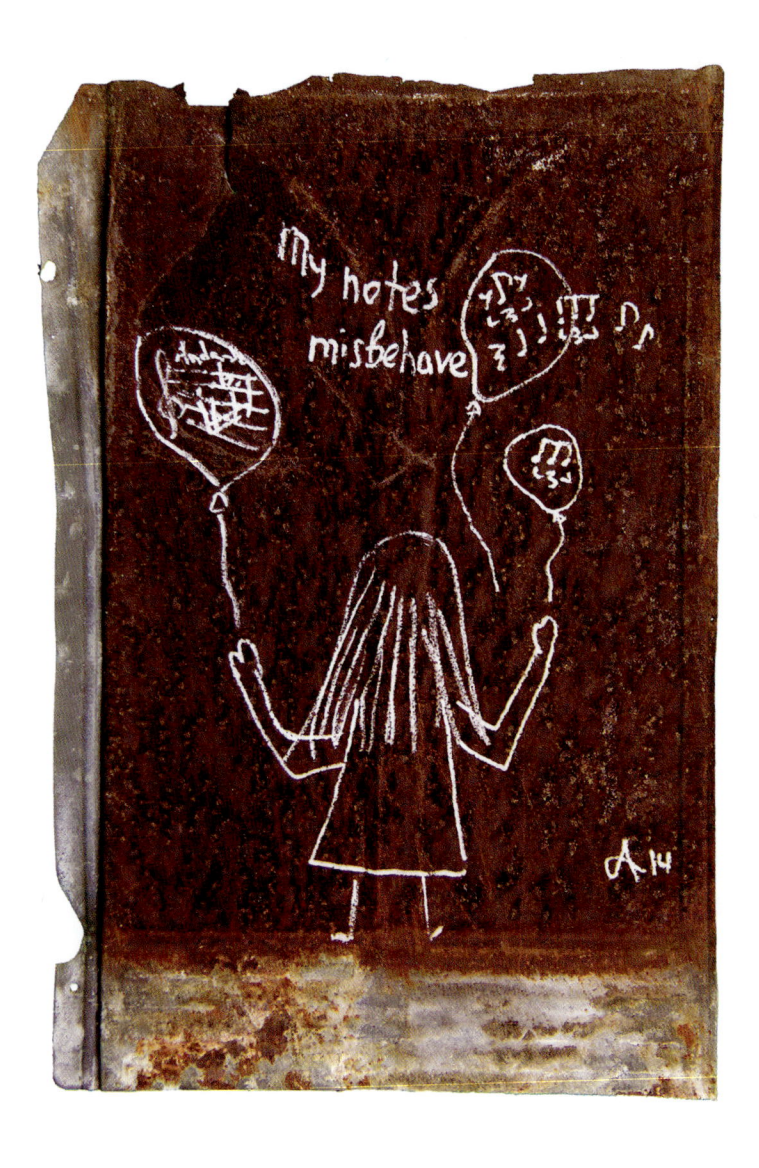

◎

I never know what to say when asked about my occupation. "Occupation" – such a strange word! How can one occupy a profession? And does it imply that you are forcefully taking someone else's space to which you have no right? Suddenly, your job takes the form of a war zone, and you stand alone and lost, staring at a hostile blank page.

◎

There are only
two types of composers:
composing composers
and decomposing composers.

36 EXCESS OF BEING

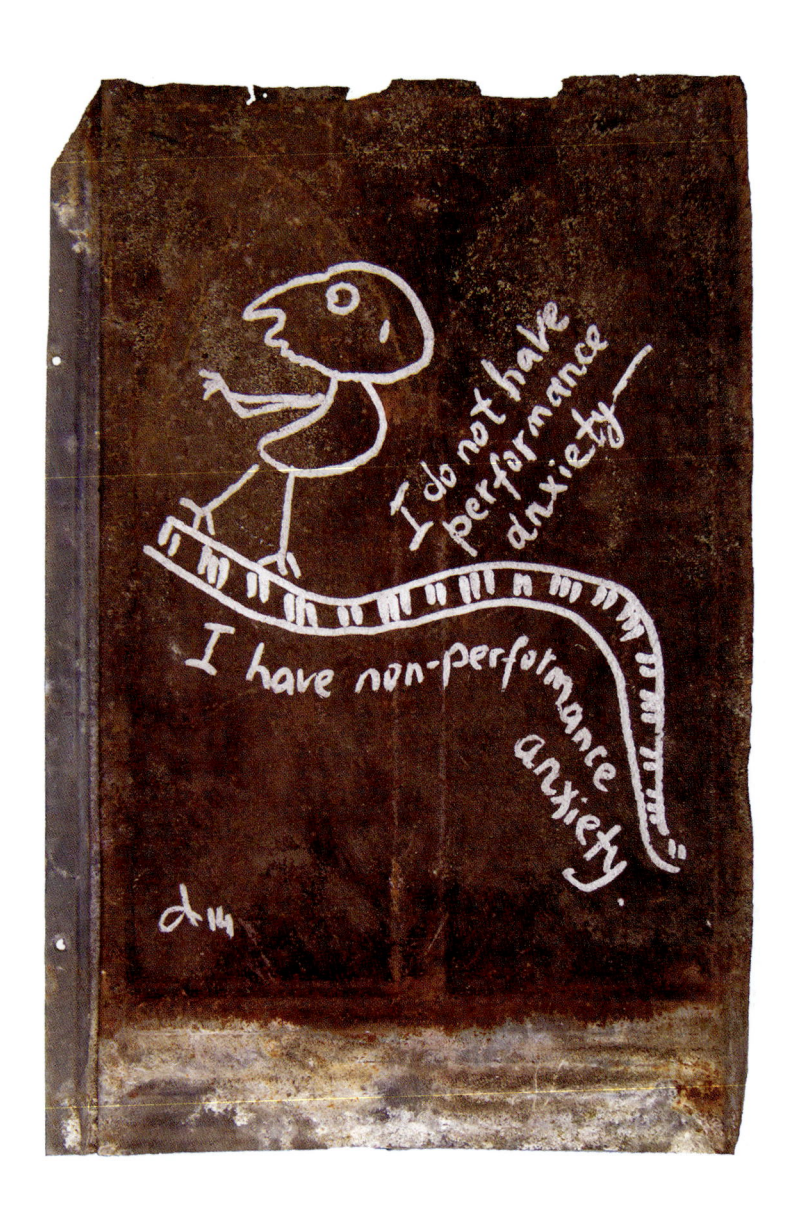

◎

During a concert, everything becomes irrelevant – your health, your conflicts, your ambitions… You dissolve in music and only music remains. Then life starts again. You return to reality, feeling emptied yet grateful. Grateful emptiness.

◎

On the compositional process:
I dream,
then dissect the dream
into sounds,
translate the sounds into symbols,
which can resurrect the dream.
Bound to the page
it's a shadow of itself,
but only by looking at shadows
we are not blinded
by light.

◉

World premiere:
If it goes well, all the glory is for the performer.
If it goes wrong, all the blame is to the composer.

◉

I
notate
silences.

◉

One of my friends, a violinist, once said to me: "I love giving world premieres. Playing a new piece for the first time is like making love to a virgin." I replied: "Just make sure you are not going to break her heart by not returning to her again and cheating with the next world premiere, or, even worse, with an old-world whore."

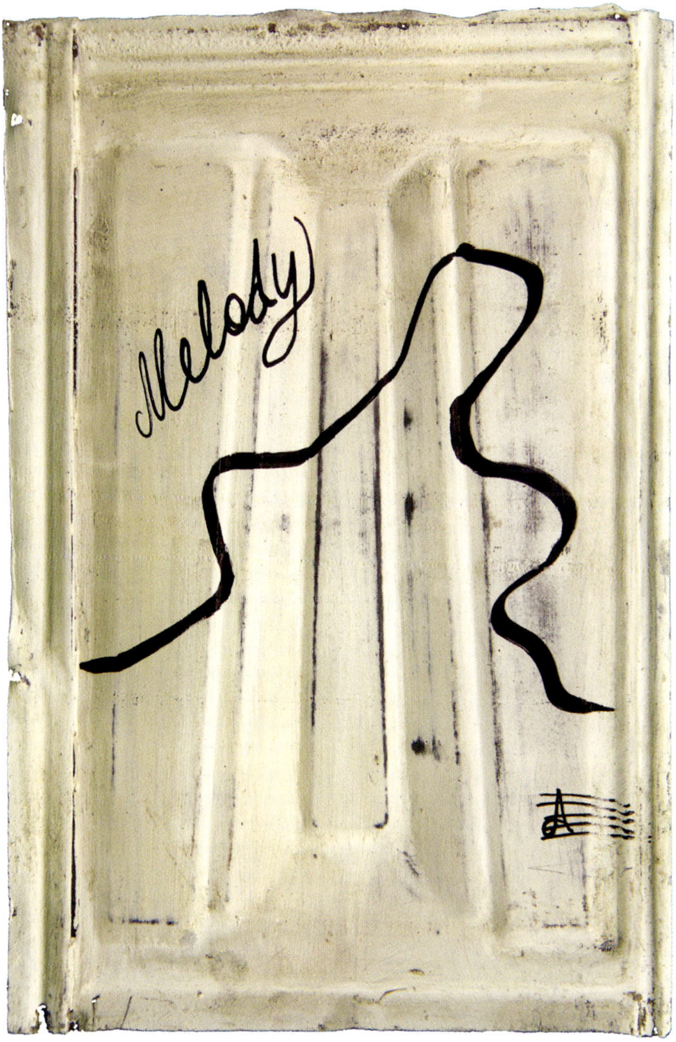
Melody

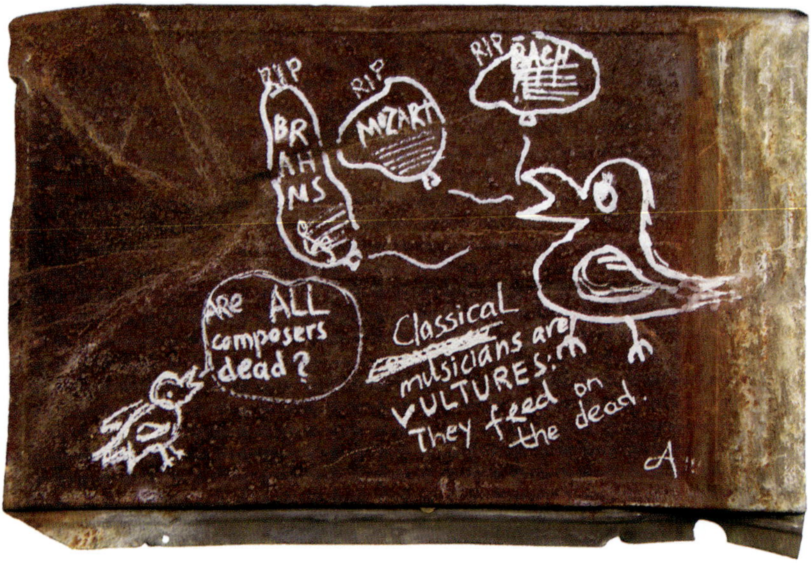
RIP
BR AH MS
RIP
MOZART
RIP
BACH
Are ALL composers dead?
Classical musicians are VULTURES: They feed on the dead.
A

Possession of a bird
doesn't guarantee
possession of a song.

I'm led by ear.
Noise overwhelms me.
It's *all* noise.

If showing up is 80% of success, not showing up sometimes results in 100%.

42　Excess of Being

◉

I work on surviving my work.

◉

Telepathy works in traffic and chamber music.

◉

We can best teach that which we do not naturally possess – sharing the weak links.

Finally, at peace,
I listen to the *other* silence –
the one that wells up
from within.
Finally, I'm listening.

To a critic: I'm so glad you noticed all my imperfections. They are my best features.

On compositional technique: Leave the recipe in the kitchen.

IF YOU HAVE a FLAW — MAKE it part of your LEGACY.

◎

The photographer tried to prettify me for the photo shoot. "I bite!" I growled in response.

◎

I get nervous on the day of performance. Unfortunately, every day is a performance.

◎

S. is too famous but not famous enough.

Mistakes are the cracks in the walls of your prison.

Music happens within. A performer allows others to hear what is already sounding.

Be respectful to your Muse. She can hear you.

48 Excess of Being

Possession of a bird doesn't guarantee possession of a song.

◎

Musicologists sometimes forget that I am a composer and take me as their own.

◎

Feeling sad after this glorious sunset: I will never be able to create anything like it.

◎

An *a priori* forgettable concert.

◎

I'm no longer interested in hearing yet one more polite performance. Give me roughness, risk-taking, even vulgarity, just not politeness. Composers bleed their lives into music. The least performers can do is to remove their safety shields.

◎

This is your solo. Don't tiptoe around it.

◎

Patrons are welcome, patronizing – not.

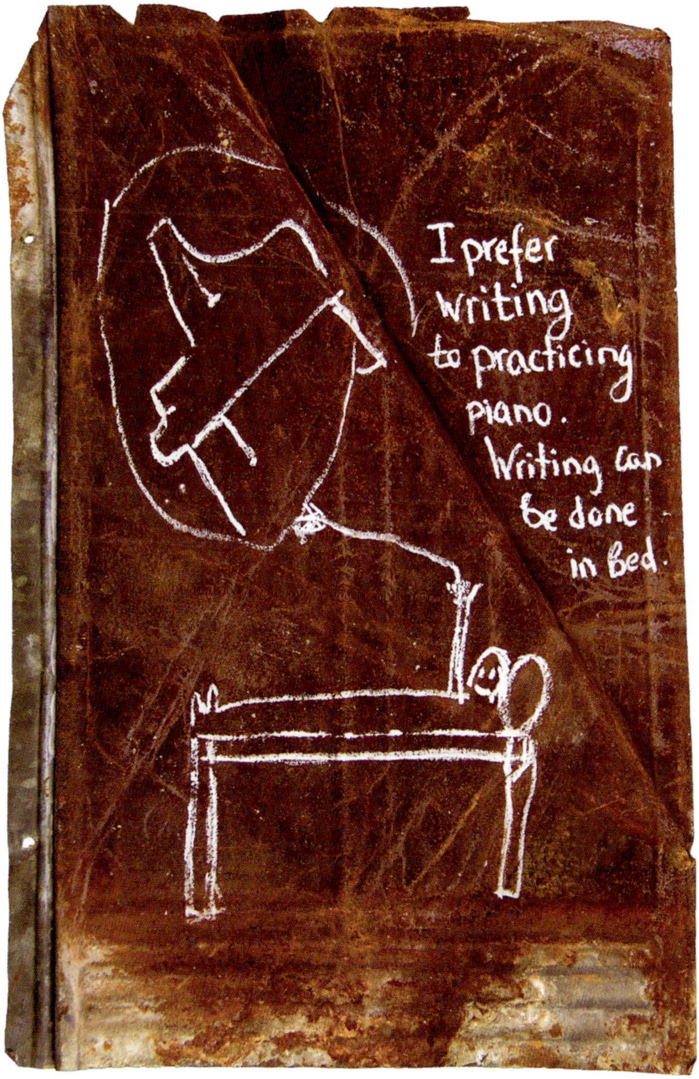
I prefer
writing
to practicing
piano.
Writing can
be done
in bed.

◎

I capture rapture.

◎

I'm replaying my pause in a loop.

◎

Just remember – anything with strings attached sooner or later will make a sound.

Being passionate about your work is 80% of success, but passion must be sustainable for a lifetime. Otherwise it's just an infatuation.

Human is my second language. My first language has always been Music.

Don't borrow or steal – own;
Don't quote – claim;
Don't call – name;
Don't pretend – become.

◉

My first music composition teacher once advised me: "You should work quickly, but without rushing." Nowadays I compose slowly, but rush all the time.

◉

I have an unusual sense of smell. I can even smell music. Sometimes in my dreams music is sounding through the smell, through the colors, and I feel – blissfully – how everything connects, how this universe is just one alive being.… Then I wake up and all breaks apart; I'm playing with the shards and inwardly crying.

Musings 55

This music is my own, but I do borrow 12 notes.

Collaborators are usually partners in the crime of achieving a compromise.

Getting further lost doesn't guarantee getting closer to being found.

※

String instruments are like wine: They become either sour or priceless with age.

Pianos are similar to humans: Their average active life is approximately 70 years. They get ill and require transplants; some keep their magic well into old age while others lose their charms as they mature.

Brass instruments don't get old – they get recycled. An old violin bow (a thin wooden stick with horse hairs) can cost more than the entire brass section of the orchestra. A child could break the bow.

We wear heavy armor to appear strong, but only those who are not afraid of being vulnerable possess real strength.

◉

Don't bask in obscurity.

I have so much on my plate that I lost my appetite.

If you are lost
inside a labyrinth,
stop walking –
Fly.

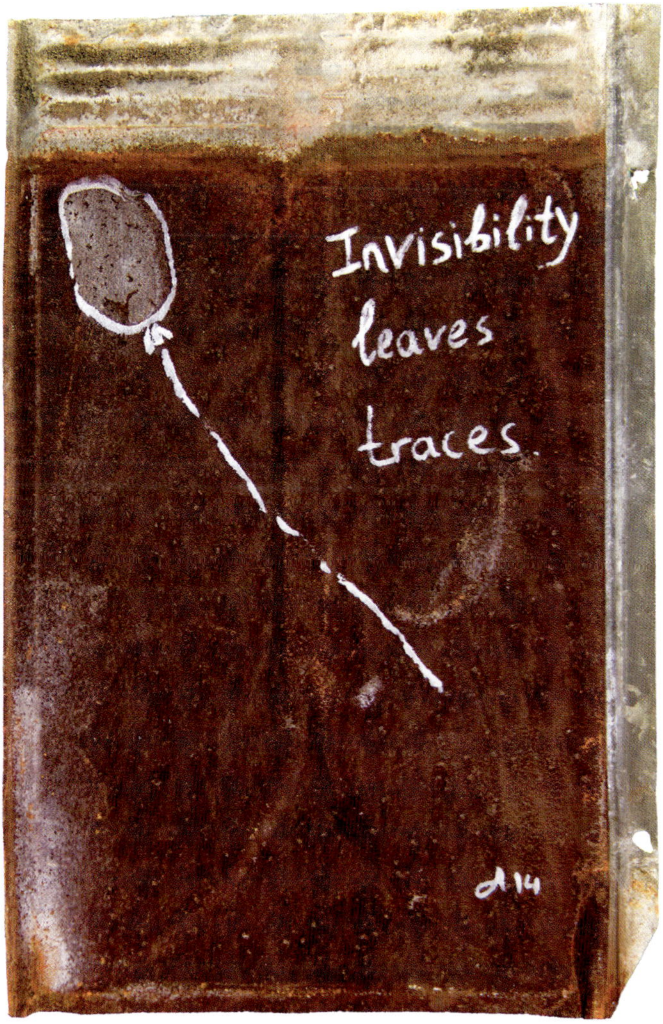
Invisibility
leaves
traces.

Marginals

on writing, readership and art

◎

When words are few, each finds its place. It's easy to get lost in a crowd.

◎

Aphorisms are samples of what this book could have been.

◎

Aphorism: an afterthought of a preconception.

An aphorism is the epitaph to a thought.

Aphorisms: spam of a writer with a short attention span.

Aphorisms: punch lines, aimed not at the reader, but at the author.

LONG FACES
grow
LONGER
redding
LYING
phrases.

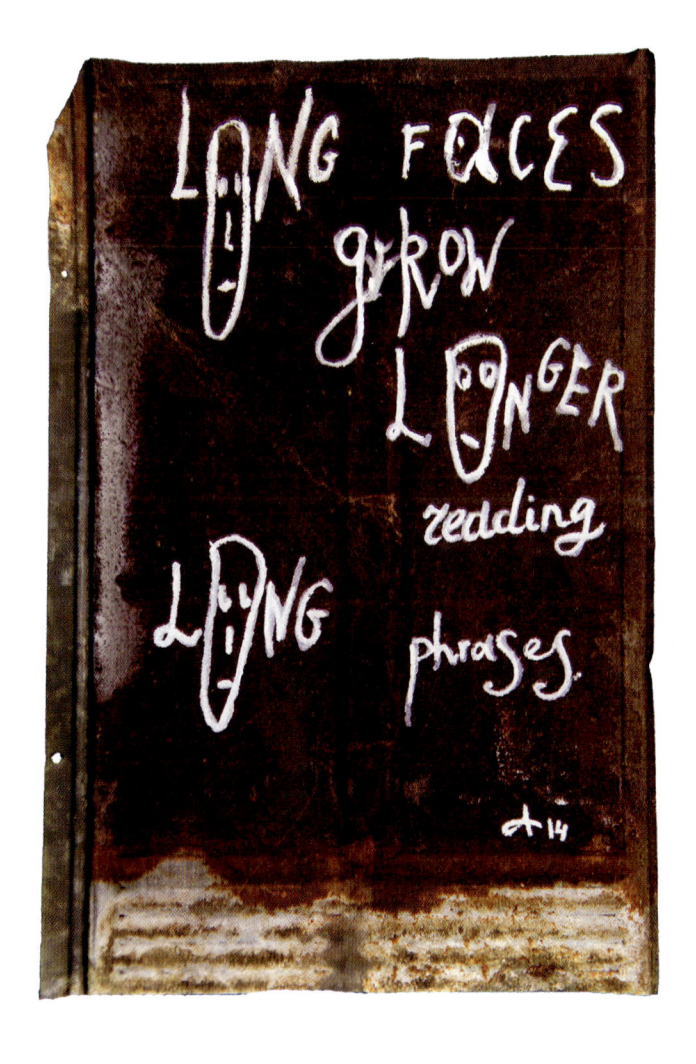

◎

Note: My best thought just evaporated.

◎

Aphorism: an appetizer without a meal to follow.

◎

Aphorism: a prelude to a canceled sermon.

MARGINALS 67

Aphorisms are commonplace oddities.

An aphorism has the urgency of a crisis, condensed into a spell against impending disaster.

Daily doses of aphorisms have severe side effects.

Marginals 69

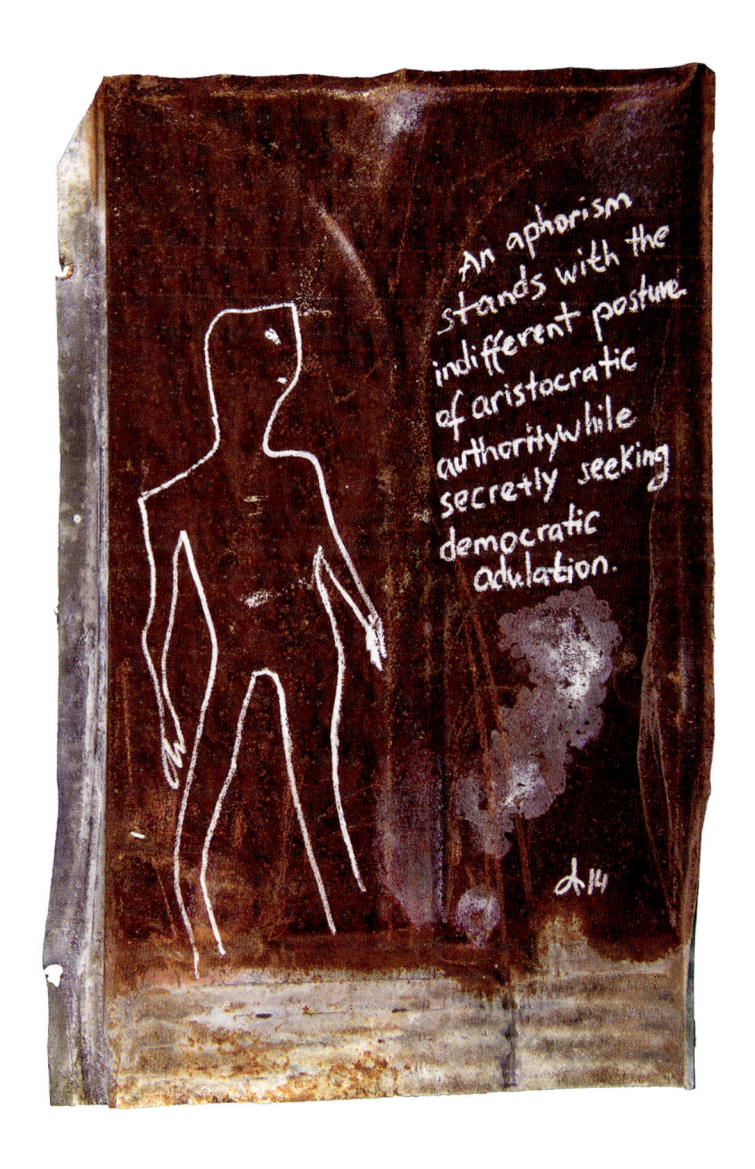

An aphorism stands with the indifferent posture of aristocratic authority while secretly seeking democratic adulation.

Aphorism: a rescued footnote for lost text out of context.

Aphorisms: self-important writing whose only value is its brevity.

Aphorisms: naked prose.

❡

An aphorist has an affair with literature, but not a decent one.

❡

Any aphorism can and will be used against its author.

❡

Aphorisms are larger than they appear.

Aphorism has been the only literary form so far mostly avoided by women. Did I just open Pandora's box?

Be polite: Pick up after your aphorisms.

Danger! Unleashed aphorisms.

Marginals 73

An aphorism isn't a cure but might be a cause.

Aphorism: a fortune cookie minus the cookie.

Aphorism: a fortune cookie minus the fortune.

WRITING ABOUT GHOSTS doesn't turn you into Shakespeare

Book of aphorisms: mausoleum of thoughts.

Writing aphorisms as a way to navigate through a crisis – condensing each experience to a sentence in order to gain distance from it.

A book of aphorisms amounts to numerous multiplications of one.

Classifieds: aphorisms in search of their author.

Classifieds: life's wisdom for sale.

An aphorism is the opposite of a poem: a destination without a journey, an answer without a question. It crawls instead of flying; it reveals instead of concealing; it betrays itself even before it's written.

Warning: These aphorisms are contagious. If you get infected – don't panic, just turn on the TV. A couple of hours of watching will cure you.

Decided to write down all my thoughts and then separate the good from the bad. Later had to revise this plan and separate the bad from the worst.

Dozing from an overdose of aphorisms.

MARGINALS 79

Dozing from an overdose of aphorisms

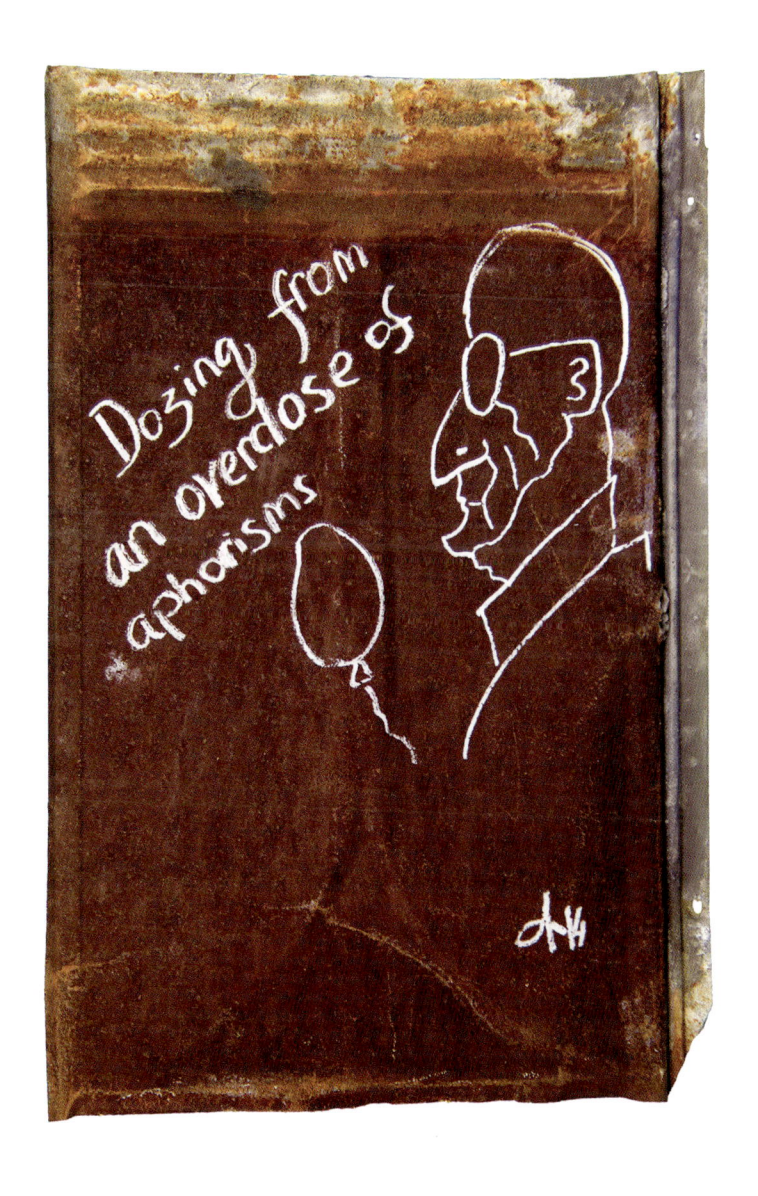

◎

    Proverb is the twin of Aphorism. While Aphorism inserts itself in society, Proverb prefers the countryside and a simpler way of living.
    Epigram is the wife of Aphorism: charming, but easily dismissible.
    Epitaph is the mother of Aphorism: Her faults may be many, but it would be unthinkable to disapprove without risking being disinherited.

◎

An aphorism stands with the indifferent posture of aristocratic authority while secretly seeking democratic adulation.

◎

Reading aphorisms by living authors can be infuriating. Who do they think they are?

❂

This book is a collection of footnotes to my life.

❂

These thoughts have occurred to many people and for a very long time. I just happened to write them down.

❂

This is a book by a venting introvert.

◎

Who knows what your thoughts are doing with my thoughts while we are innocently asleep?

◎

I'm not denouncing my writing; I'm just joining its opposition.

◎

I never planned to write this book, but this book had other plans.

MARGINALS 83

It's easier to cut than to edit. Off with her head!

Artist is the chronographer of Time.

Stage exit: I'm gone forever. Continue as before.

Excessive perfectionism metastasizes into chronic procrastination.

Stay above your circumstances whenever you can, especially whenever you can't.

This is a pot of plot.

If there is consensual love, there must be consensual art, but great art is never consensual. (You may deny your lover, but you can't deny your calling.)

My spelling is spellbound – nothing is what it seems.

Creating and lovemaking are similar – if you overanalyze the process, you will never be great at it. You need to give yourself wholly and be carried to the other side of oblivion.

◉

I do not stretch my imagination – my imagination stretches me.

◉

Lying is not a synonym for creative thinking.

◉

A writer's job includes disentangling past from future.

Quotation marks are imaginary sneers.

Design is not art: Useful art does not exist.

You don't have to be a perpetual rebel to feel relevant. Sooner or later, someone will rebel against your rebellion.

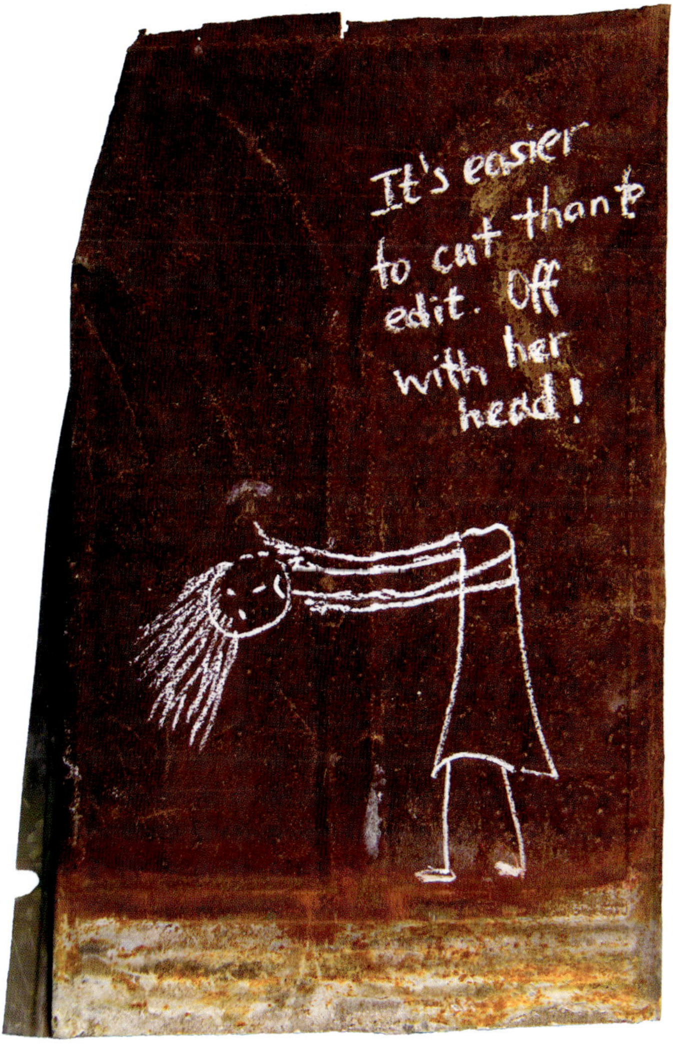
It's easier
to cut than to
edit. Off
with her
head!

❁

About one-third of all great Russian poets and writers were imprisoned. The Russian government has always been generous in broadening its writers' experiences.

❁

Poetry happens.

❁

Prison happens.

❂

What do you do for a living? I give form.

❂

I collect souls. No, not dead souls, but living souls. All encased and preserved, ready for dissection: I'm a writer.

❂

Advisory board conditions: I can be involved, but only if I don't have to be involved.

Music: illusion of the best kind.
Life: illusion of the worst kind.
Literature: the border zone between the two illusions.

Writing a lot doesn't guarantee that you have written anything.

Cold pizza for breakfast: writer on a deadline.
Breakfast in the afternoon: writer without a deadline.

◉

Objective adjectives do not exist.

◉

I have a big following, especially with the mosquito population.

◉

On life, love and art:
Let it be – and it will flourish.
Will it to be – and it will suffocate.
Make it – and it will never be born.

Our only limitations are the limitations of our language.

Art creates Time.
Time creates Art.

It's not fully yours
until you have shortened it.

❂

You can enchant a great poem into existence;
you can conjure it,
you may even dream it into being,
but you can't manufacture it.

❂

I don't like italics – they are too loud.

❂

I'm always misquoted, even in the original.

96 Excess of Being

> When words are few, each finds its place.
>
> It's easy to get lost in a crowd.

◎

Form and content are like a long-married old couple: One rarely survives without the other.

◎

I feel like a trespasser in my own book.

◎

No, my English is not British or American: It's self-made.

◉

The eyes of my readers leave bruises on my skin.

◉

Me, Myself and the Other argued about who had written this book. Decided to wait and see. If successful – I will share the credit with Myself; if a failure – it's all the Other's fault.

◉

This book is
imaginary.
You are holding
spaces
between the silences.

◎

Don't tear pages from my life.

◎

I left my punctuation in the second glass of wine

◎

Every book is just that – a collection of words, random findings in which memories hide.

◎

I'm only professional at procrastinating. Everything else is a hobby.

◎

I'm not a highbrow artist. I'm not even a lowbrow. I pluck my brows.

◎

My perfect nightmare would be to think in aphorisms *all* the time.

Disclaimer: I have illegible writing, which results in incomprehensible reading.

The best if-isms start with "What if…"
The worst if-isms start with "If only…"

Writing about ghosts
doesn't turn you
into Shakespeare.

◉

I'm not holding the copyright – the copyright is holding me.

◉

If you survived this far, it doesn't mean that you are flourishing.

◉

His job description included finding the word "preëminent" in any article and adding umlauts above the second "e."

◎

I'm writing down my thoughts so I don't have to think them anymore.

◎

My thoughts are itching to be written; if I don't give them some ink now, there will be blood later.

◎

I'm the proud author of my undoing.

I LEFT my punctuation in the second GLASS of wine

◉

Let it go.
The work is not
yours anyway.
It has never been.
You are only
its guardian.

◉

I don't know why my characters behave the way they do. Ask them.

◉

In the right frame of mind, prose becomes poetry.

◉

Never trust
a writer of fiction
or a fictional writer.

◉

A good read doesn't equal a good book,
but a good book is always a good read.

◉

An artist should never avert his gaze. Look at it. However awful it may be, it's life, real life in all its majestic and gory glory. What do you see? What do you see? Now, give it form.

❋

To come up with one great sentence, one needs to serve a life sentence.

❋

I am hanging on an asterisk.

❋

My thoughts do not reflect my opinions. They simply happened to pass through my head.

❂

A poet
sends messages
across the abyss
of time in hope
that someone
may receive them
on the other
side.

❂

A good editor will save you from embarrassment.
A bad editor will rob you of your mistakes.

❂

I make an average of one mistake per sentence,
but sometimes one is just not enough.

MARGINALS 109

◉

A poet
continues
dialogues
in the darkness:
answering letters
from the dead
and mailing them
into the future.

◉

I wish I could distill forever
into today,
but I can only pour
today into forever.

◉

Through porous lies the truth shimmers.

❦

If it is written down, it exists.
If not, it's only waiting to be born.

❦

My life started with an exclamation point
and shaped itself into a question mark.

❦

I don't know what any of this means –
I use words randomly.

Writing on the margins of history books doesn't mean being included in the revised editions.

If possible – don't quote me.
At the very least – don't misquote me.

To a journalist: Murderer! You've killed my context!

❋

– Reader, don't read any further.

❋

His thoughts were
so deep –
the reader
drowned.

❋

I have nothing to say. I'm a writer: I need to write to have something to say.

◎

Ideas are banging at my door, demanding entrance. I feel diminished to a gateway.

◎

My grandfather always requested that I wash my hands before touching a book. He worshiped his library. To bend a page was a sacrilege worthy of spanking. "It's only a book. It's not going to break," I would object. "Write your own books. Then see if they are breakable," he would answer.

◎

Competition for the best suicide note. The winner to be published posthumously.

ON WRITING:

To come up with ONE GREAT SENTENCE, ONE NEEDS TO serve a life sentence.

❦

I wish I could rewind my life and press delete, but I'm not the editor of my life's story. I'm not even a contributor – just an avatar.

❦

Never understood why anyone would want to write aphorisms. What a self-centered, pompous, futile form, and an instant recipe for failure.

❦

I don't like the principal character of my diary – not very believable.

◉

I have an accent in every language I write.

◉

Looking at the books in my library: Which ones will I never read? They will all outlive me. They will bear witness.

◉

Filling the void with words creates the illusion of not being alone.

◎

Hardcover books are imposing: They know they will survive you. Paperbacks are more perishable, thus friendlier. Electronic books are frightening: They are bodiless ghosts, messengers from another world. One day someone might be able to conjure you into existence with the help of some unimaginable gadget that fits under his dirty fingernail.

◎

Most people don't talk to you – they speak *at* you; when eventually they speak *through* you – you speak for them.

◎

Careful! You are drooling adjectives.

❊

I write inconsolably.

❊

Everything I've said here must have been said before by others and much more eloquently. I was just too lazy to read it.

❊

We might as well be mute. Someone for sure already used all our daily words and even their exact combinations and sequences.

◉

The difference between art and life:
art – magnifies,
life – diminishes.

◉

I
plant
weeds.

◉

Long
faces
grow
longer
reading
long
phrases.

❂

English is my second language, so these are my secondary thoughts.

❂

I-phorisms and you-phorisms happen even to the best of us.

❂

Aphorisms are both approachable and intimidating. Approachable – because you only have to write a phrase or a paragraph. Anyone can come up with a couple of sentences. Yet this brevity also casts a shadow of false self-importance. Since it stands by itself – it seems to attract the spotlight. You have nowhere to hide, and the loneliness makes you feel exposed for who you really are: just a lost child, scribbling words, then looking for their meaning and dreading that tomorrow will be less survivable than today.

If I had something better to say – do you think I'd be saying *this*?

All you do is gather material for your obituary.

Whenever you postpone something – its force of resistance becomes stronger.

❡

Some writers take themselves so seriously that they no longer can be taken seriously.

❡

Modernity is maternity – forever pregnant with the future.

❡

The future of contemporary art:
    a) It's no longer contemporary.
    b) It's no longer art.

124 Excess of Being

◉

Essential originality emerges only when it is not a goal in itself. Everything else is superficial novelty that gets old before tomorrow strikes.

◉

I tame
wild
words.

◉

You are trespassing on my thoughts! All right… go ahead, but then make them your own.

Do letters understand the meaning of the words they are making?

Writer's block: accumulated procrastination.

There is no progress in art. Art denies Darwinism. The music of Stravinsky is not better than Mozart's; Mozart is not better than Bach; Picasso is not better than Rembrandt. There is no progress – only linguistic and stylistic changes reflecting the times.

◉

I'm wearing my perspective inside out and upside down.

◉

My sculptures are beautiful: You're just looking through the wrong pair of eyes.

◉

I wish I could understand poetry.
At least my own.

❂

Journalists are fiction writers on borrowed themes.

❂

He would always open a book on the last page. One time, he opened my diary. "Didn't you know how this all ends?" I asked. "She dies!"

❂

My diary is not my reflection, but my shadow: Only contour remains.

❦

My readership has a high number of casualties.

❦

Readership – a ship of readers, all reading my book (a scene from a perfectly tailored nightmare).

❦

In my dream everything made perfect sense: I had to put my reader asleep, so he could understand my writing.

◉

I am defenseless before my reader. I stand naked while he is clothed. He knows my secrets. I don't even know his name. He resents me for wasting his time. I feel *a priori* guilty. He's free to judge. I'm constantly wounded. He's superior in his anonymity. I'm vulnerable in my openness. Yet I would not trade places. He is my convex mirror.

◉

You need some distance to get closer.

◉

Reader be grateful: This book could have been a memoir.

◉

In writing – I am my better version.

◉

I am a dragon with three heads: music, literature and art. I breathe fire and fly high. I swim with mermaids and enter dreams. And you want to duel with me?! Are you aware that my stare is hypnotic? Oh, you think I am just an inflated lizard? I guess we do have to duel, after all. Alright, then, let's have Master Time be our judge. Meet me in 300 years at St. Mark's Basilica. What? You can't stay around for so long? Sorry, I forgot, you still have your mortality.

◉

I feel weighed down by the letter "W." All the wait, the work, the World Wide Web.... The weight is doubled in "W" in comparison to any other letter. Why are there no double "I"s or double "A"s, and why "W" looks much more like two "V"s or a fallen "M" than two "U"s? Some letters have minds of their own.

Help! My computer is invaded by bugs and blogs.

We think different thoughts in different languages. We assume different personalities, dream different dreams. *Homo scriptus* is an instrument of his language.

You can have affairs with more than one language.
Just remember – adultery comes with consequences.

Marginals 133

◎

I'm neither lost nor found – I'm unbound.

◎

You're reading what? Are you sure? And I thought I was only a figment of your imagination.

◎

Biographers like to belittle their main subject; as if by domesticating their hero, they feel themselves slightly larger. What power they have, crafting the posthumous image of a person, focusing on his humanity, his failures: "He was just like us with all our imperfections and shallowness." Posthumous democracy.

❦

Altitudes of inspiration
cause
nosebleeds.

❦

The place
for good taste
is in the kitchen.

❦

I would like to start every phrase with an asterisk. It has no sound, but the word is beautiful: "asterisk" – "starry-risk." The footnote would be left to the imagination of the reader, as any explanation only clouds clarity.

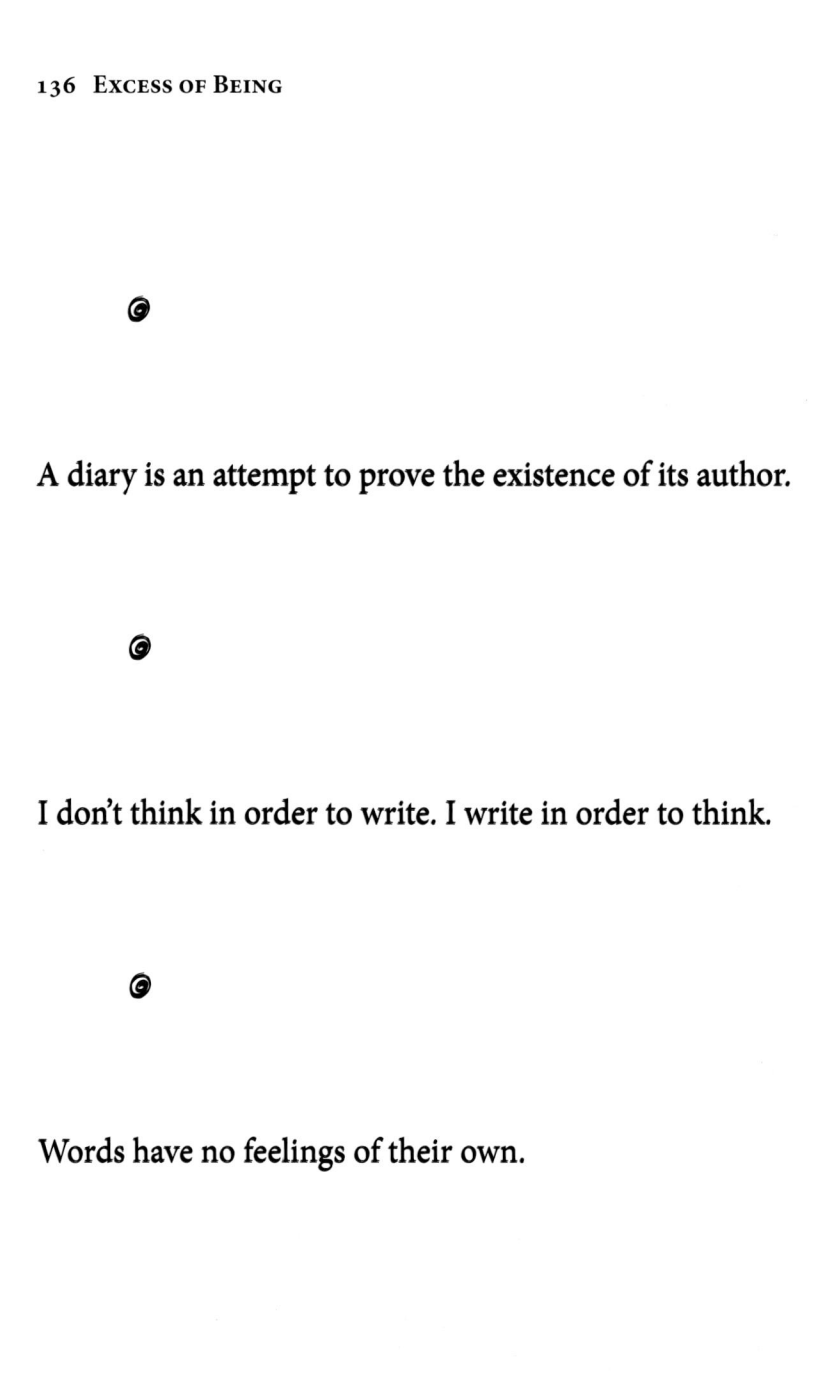

A diary is an attempt to prove the existence of its author.

I don't think in order to write. I write in order to think.

Words have no feelings of their own.

☉

The British expression "Brilliant!" rarely illuminates anything.

☉

There is no return policy on my thoughts.

☉

Eventually, what you do on paper transforms your life. Then you are no longer your own.

So, you finished your book? Congratulations! Now the fun begins. I can help you to turn it into a masterpiece. First you cut 20% of the text. It is very important. Any finished work has 20% of easily dismissible material. That's the secret of building a sustainable form: 20% has to go. Period. Don't feel sorry, you're doing yourself a favor. Well done!

Wipe off your tears and take a magnifying glass. Search for all adjectives and replace them with nouns. If you can't replace them – simply delete. Did you know that adjectives are the parasites of good prose? They are the weeds in the flowerbeds of your literary garden. Good style deserves this small sacrifice.

Delete every sentence that starts with "I." Nothing personal, but you don't want to appear selfish. Remember, this is not about you. Even if it is. With this "I" business out of the way, you are ready to send your book to the editor. When you get it back, full of red-color marking (some pages may look as if they are bleeding), try to save what is salvageable, but remember that most of the time to cut is better than to fix. Be ruthless. Brevity is a virtue and the only true consideration a writer can offer to his reader.

You may resolve that your epic novel isn't as epic as it seemed at first. Short story perhaps? With this understanding, you may want to revisit its basic premise. Maybe you might consider a prose poem – these are quite popular and can be rather successful in poetry readings. You are not planning a reading? Too bad, but now you are left with a bunch of crossed-out pages. You know it's all for the best, really. You should feel grateful. You were spared the embarrassment.

Now, with this learning experience behind, you are ready for your next yet-to-be masterpiece. Don't forget to thank your advisors in the preface. Don't feel like writing? Perhaps then you can become a critic so you can help others and return the favor. Every writer needs a friendly supportive hand. I've lent you mine. Now it's your turn.

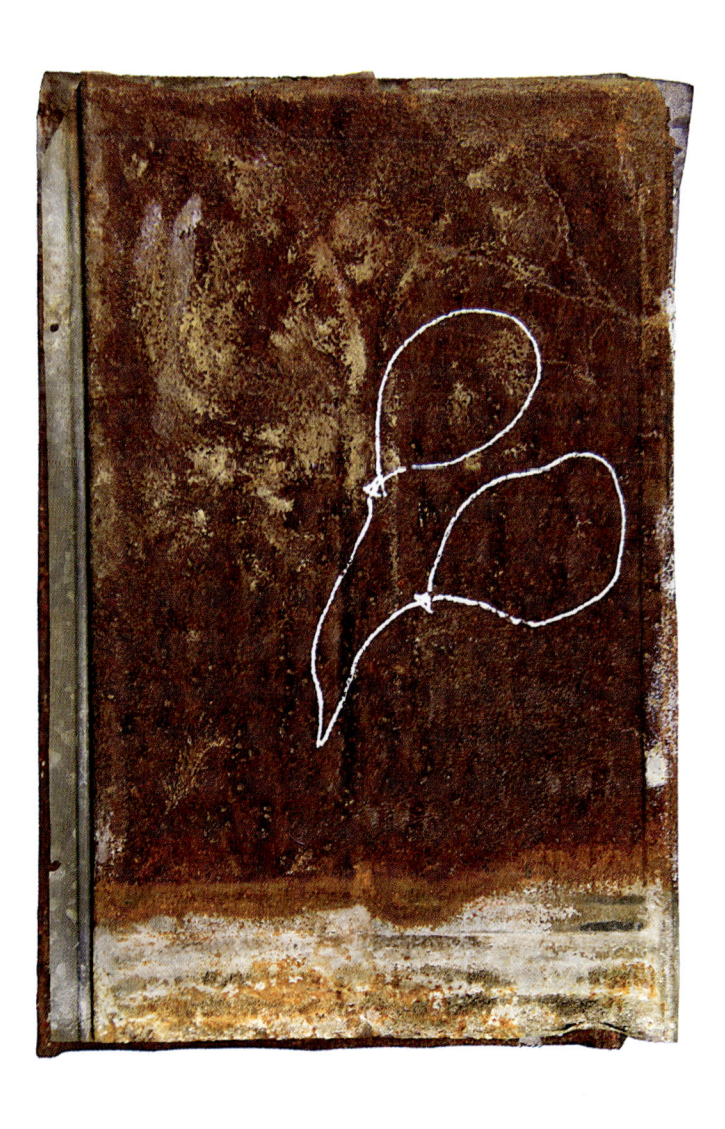

Findings

on life and other illusions

If you have been falling
for a long time –
keep on falling.
At some point,
it will be perceived
as flying.

Do not argue with idiots;
they will outsmart you.

Life is serious business. You may as well take it lightly.

You can only master something by loving it.

I am the sole survivor of my bad temper.

Wait… Lubricate this thought before penetrating my mind.

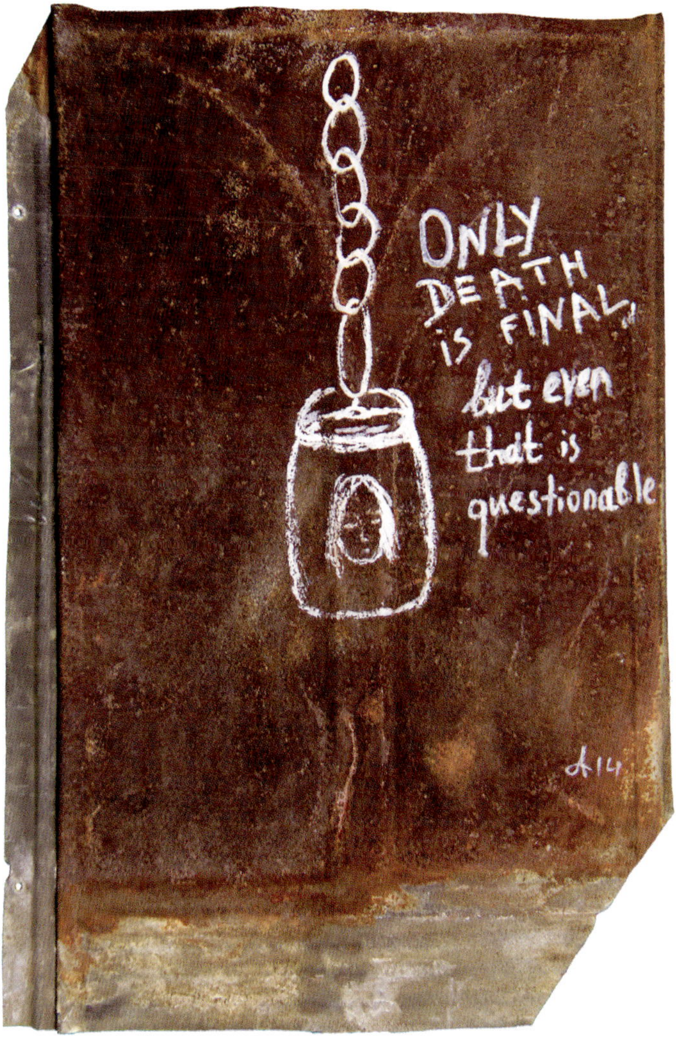
ONLY
DEATH
IS FINAL,
but even
that is
questionable

◎

I'm test-driving my limitations.

◎

If you truly desire it – it's already yours.
If it is on your wish list – it will remain there.

◎

I wish I could upgrade myself to the next version, but I'm no longer compatible with this life.

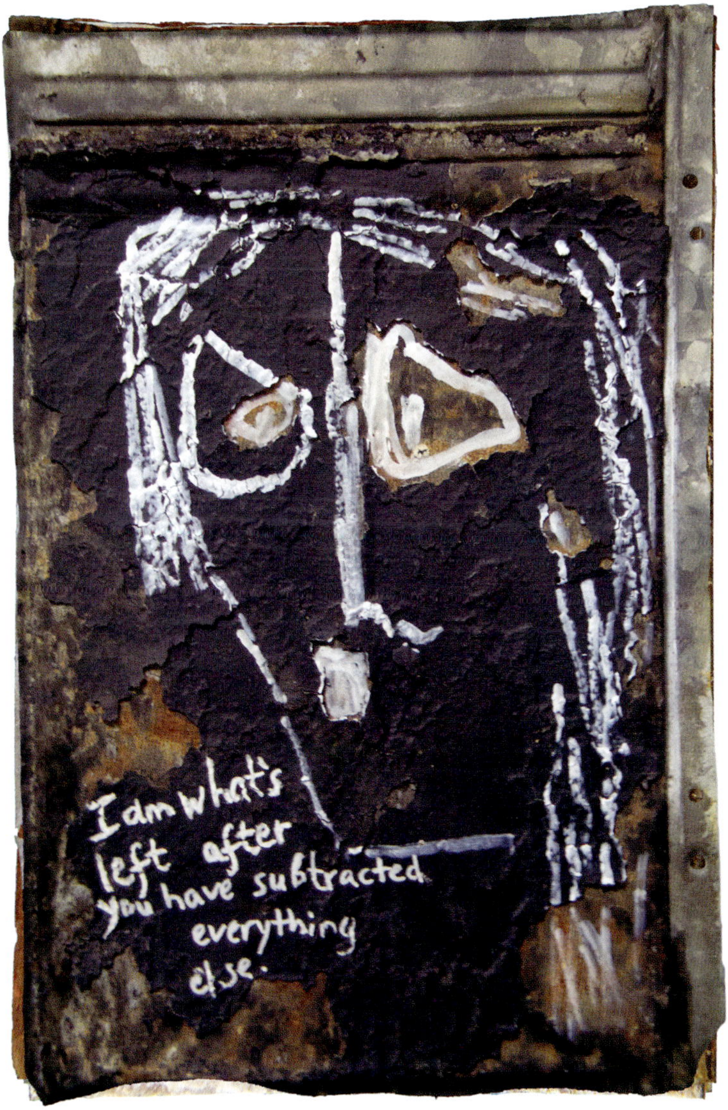
I am what's
left after
you have subtracted
everything
else.

❦

Sorry, but my circumstances are circumcised.

❦

It's all just too much to bear!
Especially that which is too little.

❦

I am what's left after you have subtracted everything else.

FINDINGS 149

◎

My shadow is not fully synchronized with me lately; there is a microsecond delay in the shadow's movement, a tiny black hole, into which things slip and disappear.

◎

Procrastination increases the gravitational pull.

◎

I wish it didn't matter what I wish.

Time doesn't heal. It simply shifts focus.

Fears, like most bullies, are cowards.

I'm only myself,
but even that is too many.

IF YOU HAVE BEEN
FALLING FOR A LONG
TIME — KEEP ON FALLING.
AT SOME POINT IT WILL
BE PERCEIVED
AS FLYING

◎

Only death is final,
but even that is questionable.

◎

If you are a big ship,
stay away from shallow waters.

◎

Large wings are not meant
for short-distance flying.

◎

Some weeds are worth cultivating.

◎

I have delusions of lack of grandeur.

◎

Many men accomplish their dream of building a home, but very few succeed at living in it.

At midnight, the ruining of the day is complete.
Now I have a chance to save it.

Life is full of predictable surprises. Just when you thought it couldn't get any worse, it does, and it always comes as a surprise.

Death never disappoints.
We've heard no complaints from the dead.

Talking is easy; communicating is difficult. To communicate, you need to be able to commute.

I look forward to forgetting this.

What doesn't kill us – makes us heavier.

FINDINGS 157

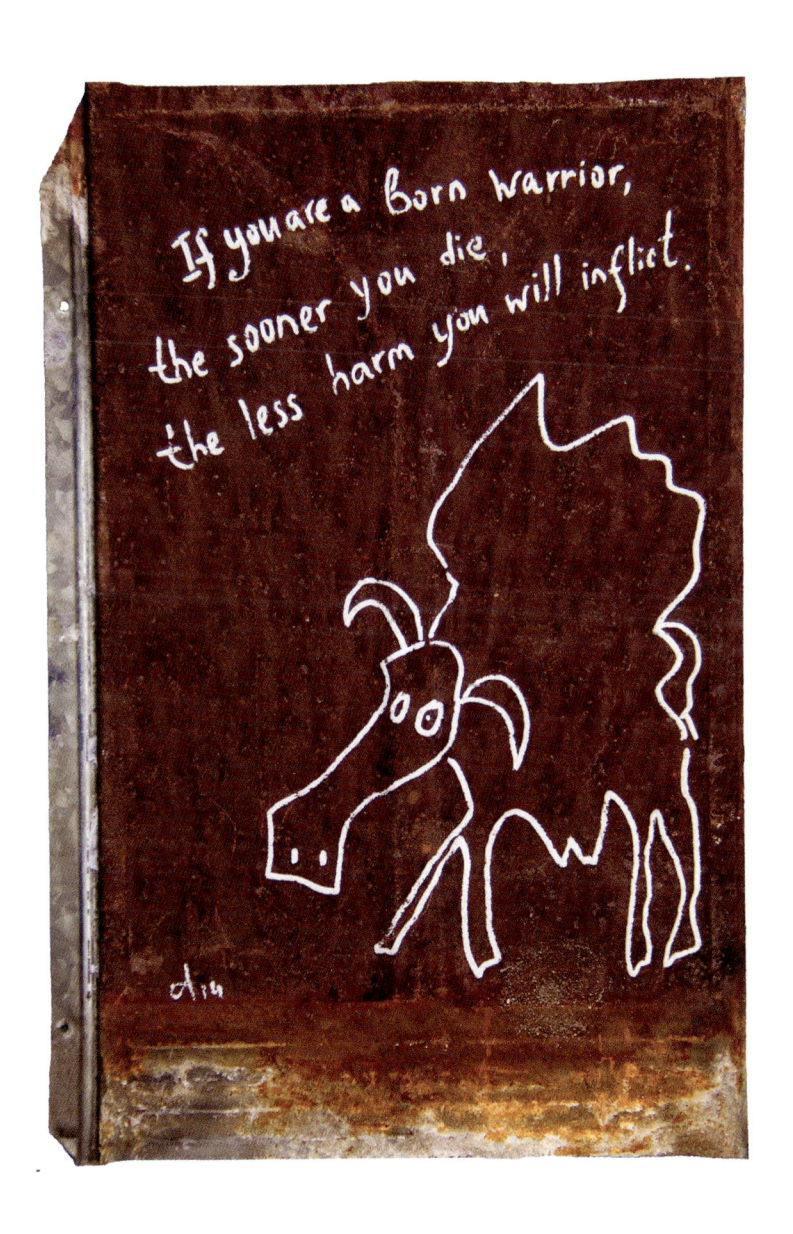

Most crimes have roots in boredom.

True passion does not care for validation.

Pleasure dilutes; pain concentrates.

◉

I am not street-smart but world-wise.

◉

Accumulated sadness feeds on desires.

◉

My brows like to comment on everything, and they never share an opinion.

◉

My highbrow advises me;
my lowbrow ridicules.

◉

Water holds reflections of those who are drinking it.

◉

He gracefully handled his disgrace.

◉

The real question is not "To be or not to be?"
but rather, "Am I?"

◉

Death defines life. I'd rather stay undefined.

◉

People who often talk of their honor are usually those who commit the most dishonorable deeds.

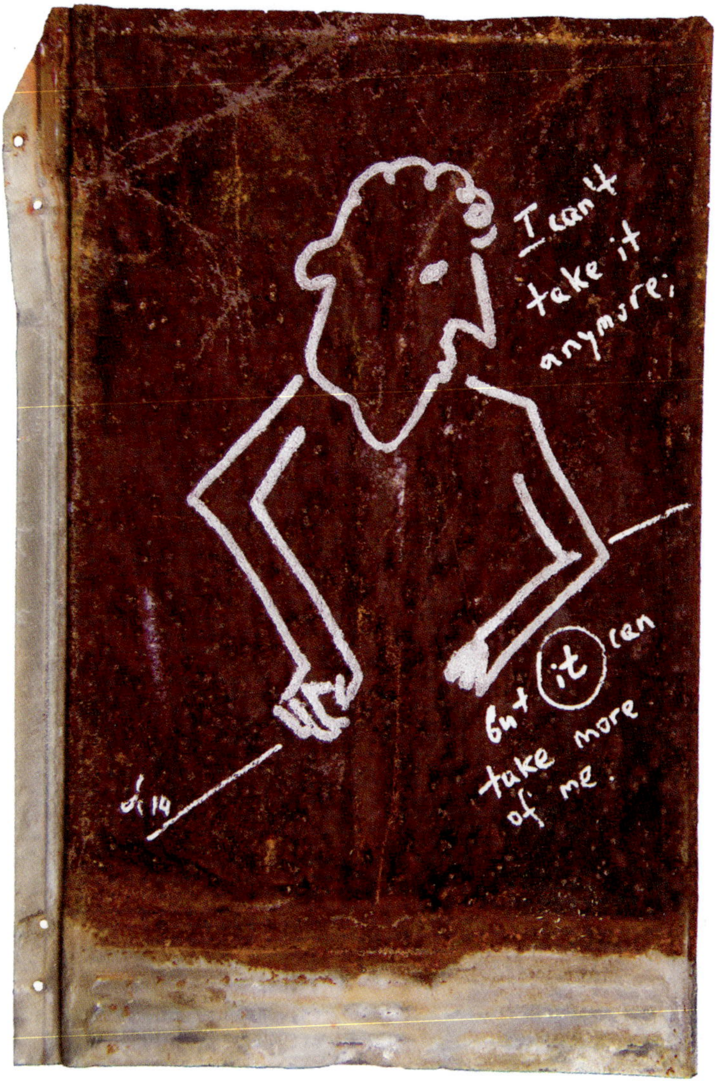
I can't take it anymore;
but it can take more of me.

The main advantage of youth is its ignorant fearlessness, which can be more powerful than all of the combined wisdom and experience of old age.

The news is too noisy to let in.

Social refinement doesn't equal good taste.

❦

Be wary of anyone who prides himself on his ideals, for he will certainly sacrifice you to them.

❦

I have inflammation of the imagination.

❦

Times rarely change, but our scars weigh us down.

◎

My train of thought lost its operator.
Collision is inevitable.

◎

How soon will you forget reading these lines?
How soon will you forget about forgetting them?

◎

A child grows much faster than his parent.

You can be brutally honest, but it doesn't mean that what you are saying is true.

The bright future was just a step ahead of him until it became just a step behind.

Judgmental righteousness is a sure sign of misled sheep.

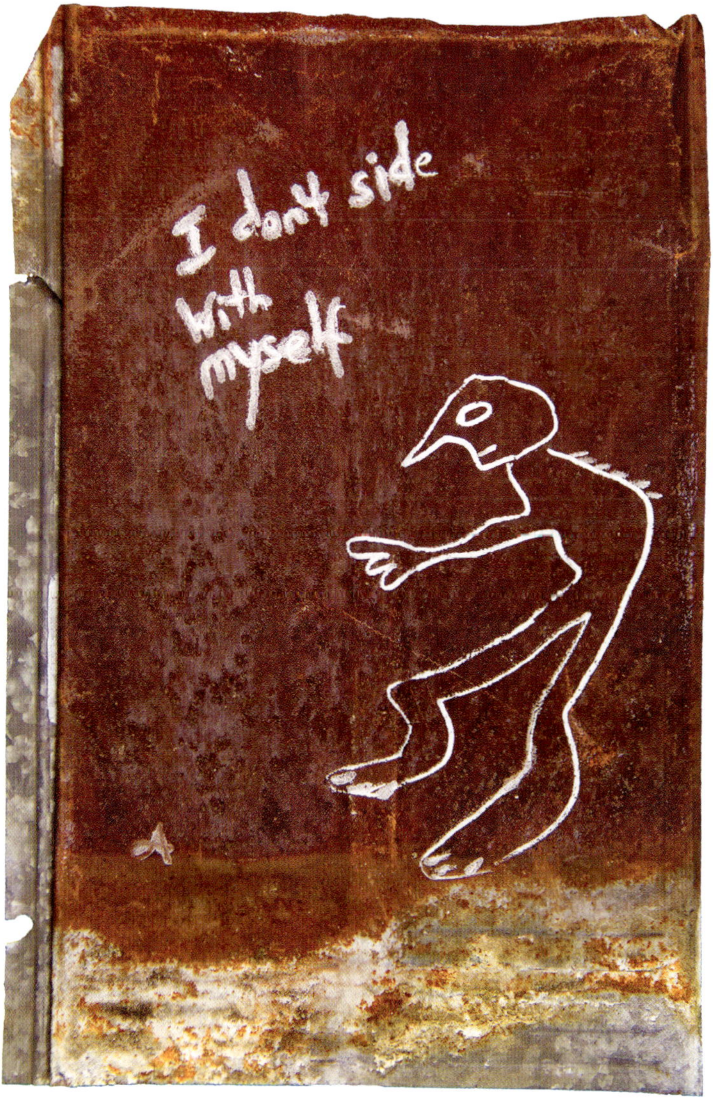
I don't side
with
myself

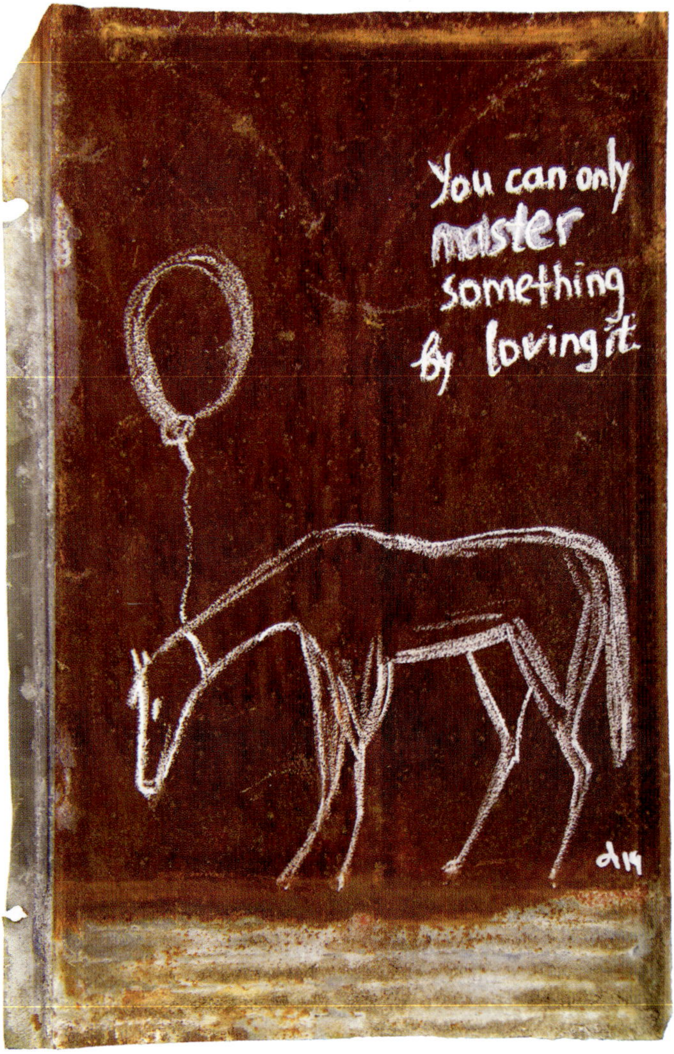
You can only
master
something
by loving it.
d14

◎

I was explaining zero multiplications to a child: "Let's say you have a hole in your pocket. This hole represents zero. You put a cookie in your pocket, but it falls through the hole, so you find no cookie, just an empty pocket with a hole. Let's say you put in a stone – same thing happens. You can put in one cent or one hundred dollars, but they all will be lost and your pocket will remain empty." The child looked at me and asked: "Can you mend my pocket?"

◎

All news is alarming.

◎

I like imaginary numbers best. All real numbers become imaginary when multiplied by "i."

Don't cushion your life with too much caution.

Possessions lead to obsessions.

Only that which is useless is truly necessary.

❂

They kept on throwing stones at him, yet were puzzled why he died.

❂

My dog is licking the nightmares off my face.

❂

All human activities gravitate toward clutter. Effortlessly, the desk becomes cluttered, the belongings, relationships, responsibilities…. I crave for less while more is spreading its web, feeding on my remaining strength.

Everything is going according to plan. I only wonder whose plan it is.

My headache is larger than my head.

I'm not concerned about my actions. It's my inactions that worry me.

All fears are imaginary, even the real ones.

❀

Pardon my appearance, but this is how I look.

❀

If you have a hyperactive imagination, it doesn't mean that what you imagine is not real.

❀

Can attention be *paid*?

❂

I know very well what good taste is. It doesn't mean that I have to like it.

❂

Sign on a trash bin: For the donations of your unsolicited advice.

❂

How does one define virtual reality, if it is capable of directly affecting one's physical life and if one spends more time online than with friends and family? Which is the virtual reality then? And where is its virtue?

◉

Me, Myself and the Other had a fight. Woke up with a bleeding nose.

◉

Me, Myself and the Other decided to part ways, but couldn't agree on directions. I am cruel to Myself. Me too. Me too.

◉

Me, Myself and the Other went for a long walk but returned too soon and not talking to each other.

I am the sole survivor of my bad temper.

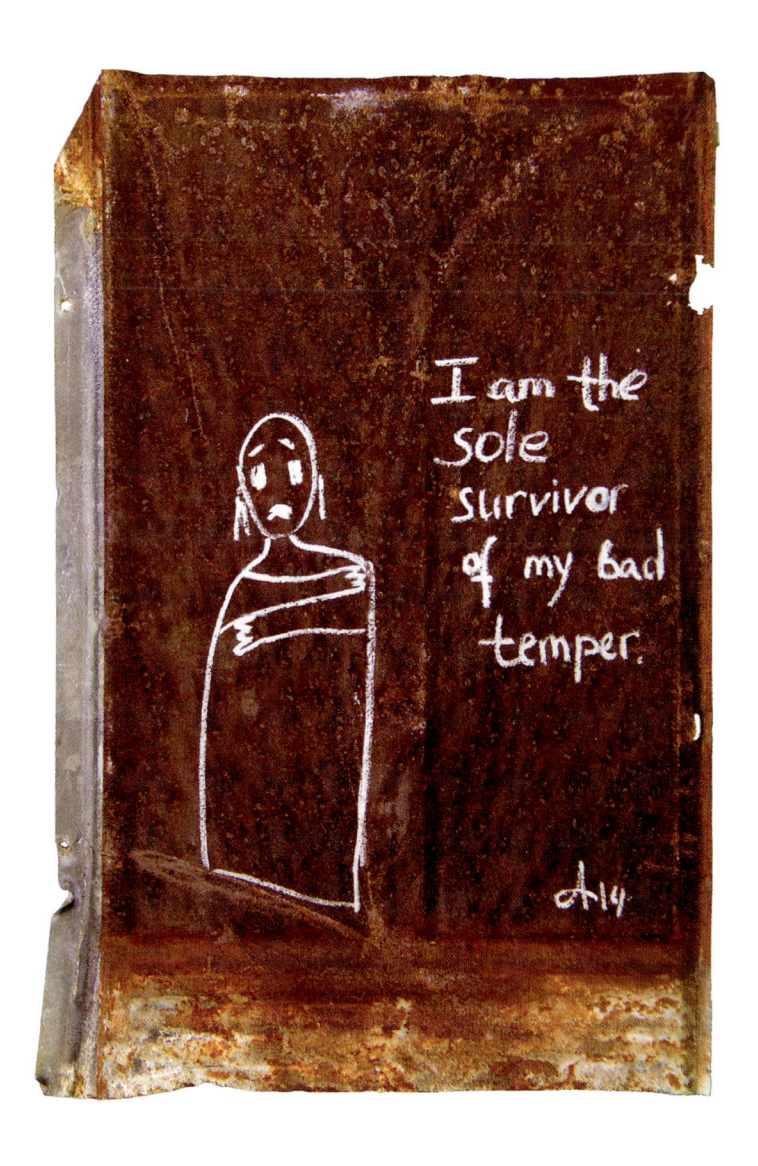

◉

Me, Myself and the Other have very different personalities. I keep on pushing Myself while the Other is just laughing at my efforts. I do all the work, but the Other gets all the credit while Myself wishes for another life altogether.

◉

I wake Myself into being, but deeply inside wonder if we both are just a dream of the Other.

◉

I often have long discussions with Myself. We never agree on anything and can get into some heated arguments. The Other just observes us quietly and smirks. I wonder if he considers us irrelevant.

❦

"Who do you think you are?" I asked Myself angrily. The Other just chuckled.

❦

Being honest with Myself hurts. I'm bruised all over. The Other watches indifferently, apparently unimpressed.

❦

Monday: I
Tuesday: Me
Wednesday: Myself
Thursday: The Other
Friday: No One in Particular
Saturday: No one
Sunday: Silence.

◎

– Is this acne?
– It is my skepticism exploded.

◎

My dog thinks that he knows best and usually does.

◎

My dog is the best part of me.

Me, Myself and the Other went
for a long walk but returned
too soon and not talking to
each other.

I would like to keep failure as one of my options. Otherwise, I feel as if I have no choice in the matter.

If I could hire you,
you would already be fired.

Help! – my past is devouring my future.

FINDINGS 185

◉

Forgive me for injuring your toes – I thought these were my stepping-stones.

◉

All fears are imaginary, even the real ones.

◉

There is too much of me around to leave me alone.

Findings 187

many men accomplish their dream of building a home, but very few succeed at living in it.

Time becomes relevant when it transcends into timelessness.

There is a certain satisfaction in feeling miserable. At least you know exactly where you stand.

The grand total is never simply the sum of its parts.

FINDINGS 189

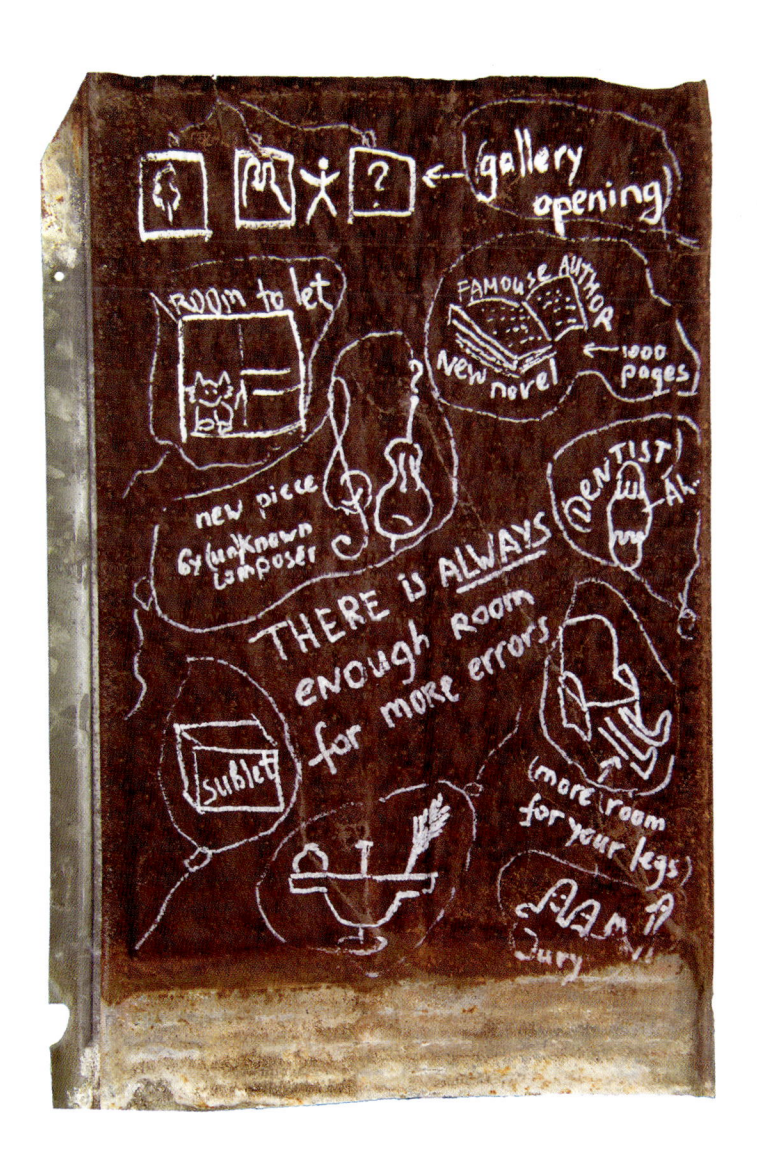

In Russian, "loneliness" and "solitude" are the same word – *odinochestvo*. Yet loneliness is a curse while solitude is a blessing. Deficit of solitude results in excess of loneliness.

Of course I'm self-destructive. If I don't stop myself, who will?

I'm weary of polished bright surfaces. I have to fight a naughty voice inside, daring me to leave my greasy imprints all over.

◉

After a while, there is no longer "after a while."

◉

If it's too shameful to leave behind – carry it proudly in front.

◉

Packing is the art of visualizing time while expanding space.

Hopes are fears in disguise.

I used to think that my life was developing in a spiral motion until I realized it had been a vortex.

Sometimes I'm brutally honest with myself, but most of the time – just brutal.

FINDINGS 193

Skepticism is the self-defense of fear.

Sarcasm is the self-defense of despair.

I wish I didn't have to deal with myself: impossible character!

Mass and mess have a tendency to accumulate.

I've been keeping a diary since I was eight years old, but always feel the discomfort of a spiritual striptease. I don't like my reflections through the mirror of a diary – all distorted. Yet I know that 15 years from now, even the worst of these pages would make me despair from missing myself – this young, brooding, dissatisfied-in-everything self, constantly searching and failing in the search. I will look back at these troublesome, struggling years with nostalgic aching, because this person, which I am now, will be gone forever and would not approve of its older, surviving double.

I'm concerned about being so unconcerned about myself.

◎

Absurdity has a strong defense system – when you threaten its existence it multiplies.

◎

I'm a slave of my need of freedom.

◎

When somebody speaks on behalf of "the people," I automatically feel excluded. Surely, no one asked my opinion.

FINDINGS 197

◎

Body and mind are two political parties fighting for leadership. The last thing I need is a civil war.

◎

Don't plagiarize my afflictions.

◎

We are in constant imaginary dialogue with our surroundings. To become free from that discourse would be to obtain freedom, but we can only move as ghosts forever bound to what we know.

Keep the word 'always' out of your thoughts. As long as something is temporary – it is bearable; it is the permanency of a condition that carries hopelessness.

Don't feed your phobias or one day they will feed on you.

My handwriting reflects the fluctuations of gravity.

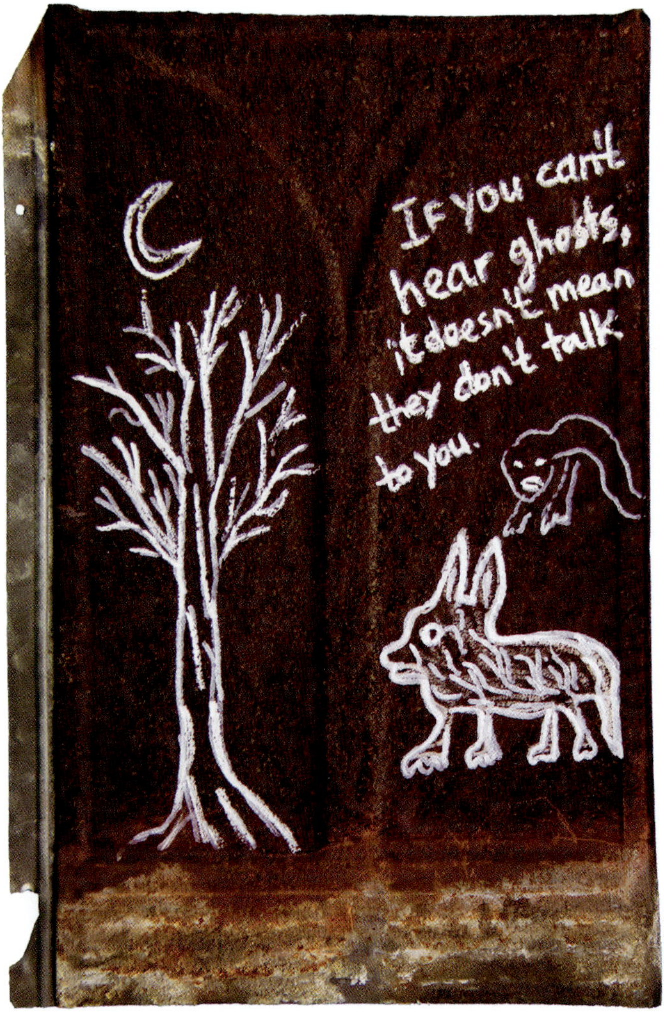
If you can't
hear ghosts,
it doesn't mean
they don't talk
to you.

◎

I have always been an outsider. That's where I belong. I'm never in. I'm always out. I'm so far out that it becomes in.

◎

I don't side with myself.

◎

Commitment is voluntary imprisonment.

❂

Life is a series of variations on a forgotten theme.

❂

The gap between good and great is much larger than between good and bad.

❂

I'm fascinated by ugliness. It's quite beautiful, really.

◎

The last straw may appear trivial and insignificant. Yet it holds all the difference between life and death.

◎

Too much understanding leads to confusion.

◎

Re-belly-on. Rebellion is fueled by an empty belly. One doesn't rebel on a full stomach.

If the journey is so important to you – reach your destination first and then journey around it.

Entrance to the shopping mall: "We consume consumers."

What we are striving for is not happiness. It's certainty.

◉

If you got it – have it.

◉

I'm past due in my present tense.

◉

My present tense is too tense.

I'm too tired to deal with things; unfortunately, things are never too tired to deal with me.

Being humane rarely defines humans.

Little savings often result in large fines.

◉

Don't play house with your landlord.

◉

Don't play doctor with your doctor.

◉

If you are a reflective surface – you remain unseen.

Be a bouncer to your emotions. Not all of them have the right to enter.

When someone tells you to have a reality check, it means he has given up on his dreams and wants you to give up on yours.

When someone tells you to grow up, it means he stopped growing himself and resents you for not following. When we don't grow – we shrink. Grow: yes, always. Grow up: never.

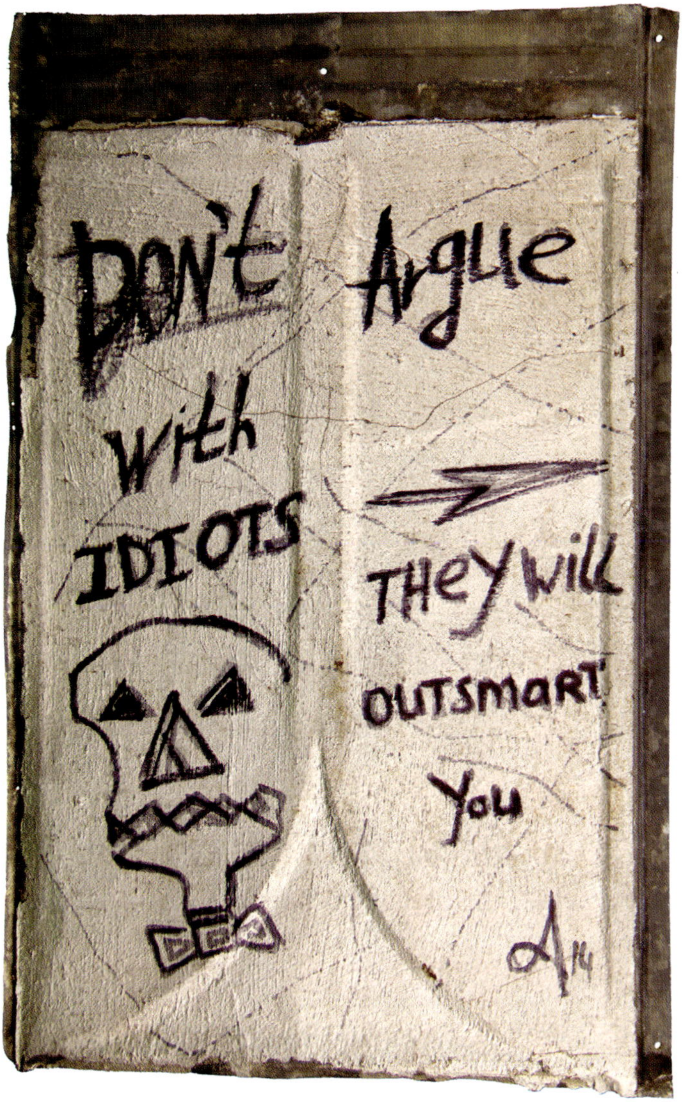
Don't Argue
with
IDIOTS
They will
OUTSMART
You

◉

I am looking at the world globe with my father. He points and says: "This is where you are."
"What do you mean? I am here with you," I respond, not understanding.
Father laughs: "You are here, but you are also there."
"You mean there is a tiny copy of me who lives there?"
"No, I mean here is there."
That did not make any sense, so I never learned geography.

◉

Many things can be too early, but only a few can be too late.

◉

Unsolicited advice results in unsolicited results.

Display of class displays the lack of class.

Misunderstanding is predetermined while understanding is coincidental.

It is when "I" is replaced by "We" that the red flag of danger arises. Suddenly you become "the other," the hunted, an outsider of the holy "We, the people." Bullies and mobs take comfort in numbers.

In the rare moments of clarity, I feel nostalgic for the present moment.

Even though I'm on the wrong side of the equation, it doesn't mean there is a right side.

I give up on catching up with myself!

I can't take it anymore, but *it* can take more of me.

Driving – bleak realities flash by brightly.

Self-pity is an indulgence, the excess of which can result in spiritual obesity with all of its deathly side effects.

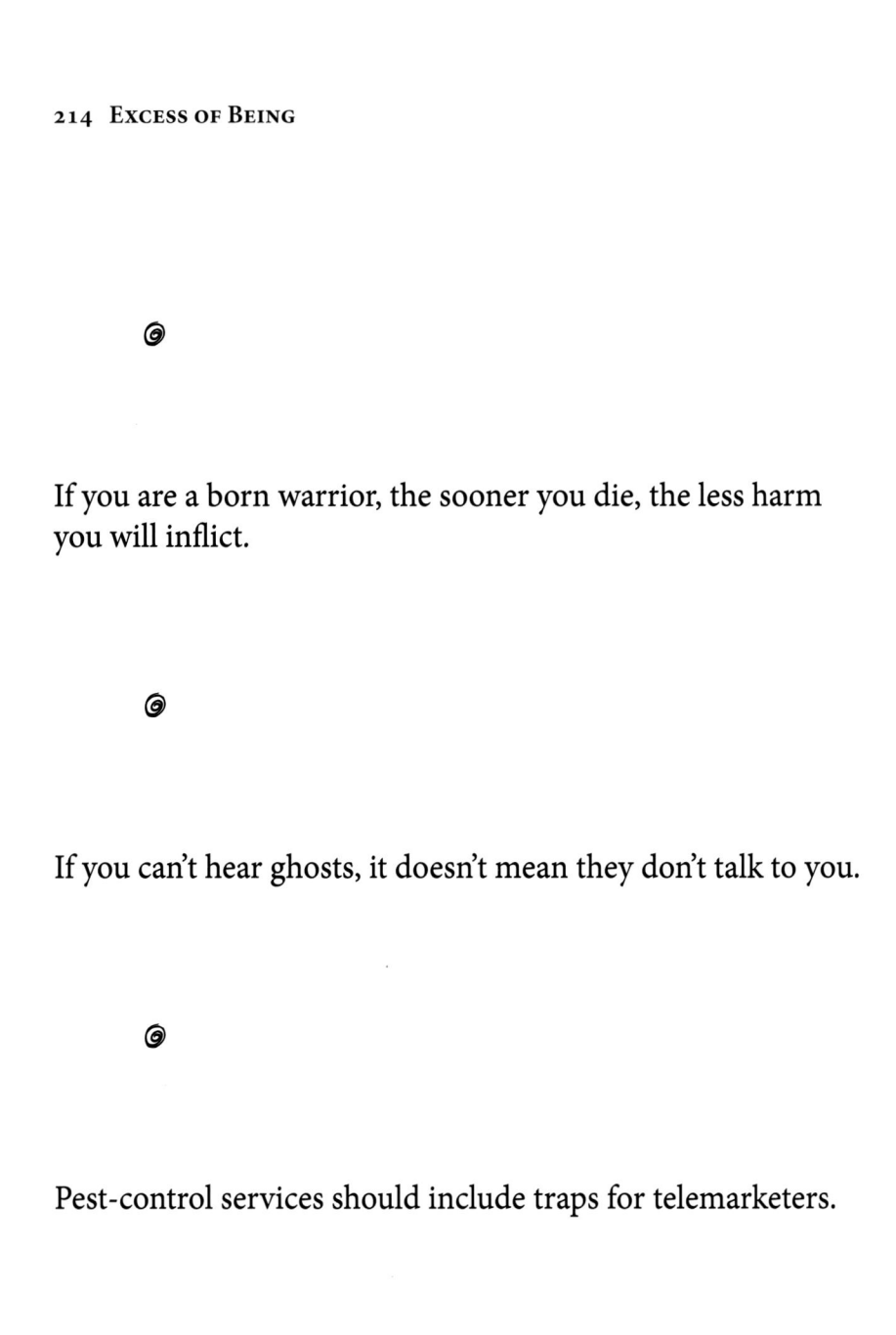

If you are a born warrior, the sooner you die, the less harm you will inflict.

If you can't hear ghosts, it doesn't mean they don't talk to you.

Pest-control services should include traps for telemarketers.

A false sense of security is still better than no security.

There is always enough room for more errors.

I am not a grown-up – I am just overgrown.

216 Excess of Being

A little revolution spices up life. A big one – burns it.

Nationalism may seem like a noble cause, but often it is the very opposite of humanism.

Emptiness seeks form.
Content seeks form.
Form seeks the transcendence of form.

◎

Emails put me in spam.

◎

If only I could avoid "if onlys" – I would be happy.

◎

Don't google my yahoo or I will tweet on you.

FINDINGS 221

At some point, you may realize that you no longer feel any need to prove anything, that you have crossed a certain border of no return and only burnt fields are around. Sometimes the best harvest is born from burnt fields.

Life is defined and divided by two objectives: striving for more and striving for less. To change gears from one to another takes courage.

Words betray their meaning. The moment we pronounce a word – we lose it forever.

◉

When depression claims your future, it is not so terrible and still can change, but when it alters your past – it is tragic.

◉

Let me say this once and for all, let me repeat it again and again – I'm not going to comment.

◉

Debating to get up or not? Gravity wins.

Barbarians have their own version of history.

I collect minuses.

Plus
is a vertical minus
on top of a horizontal minus.

❦

Pluses are the grave-markers of minuses.

❦

The lovemaking of two minuses equals a plus.

❦

Please remove your pluses. They cast shadows on my minuses.

Minus is half of a plus – its better half.

Minuses are heavier than pluses.

I am not getting old – I am getting extinct.

FINDINGS 227

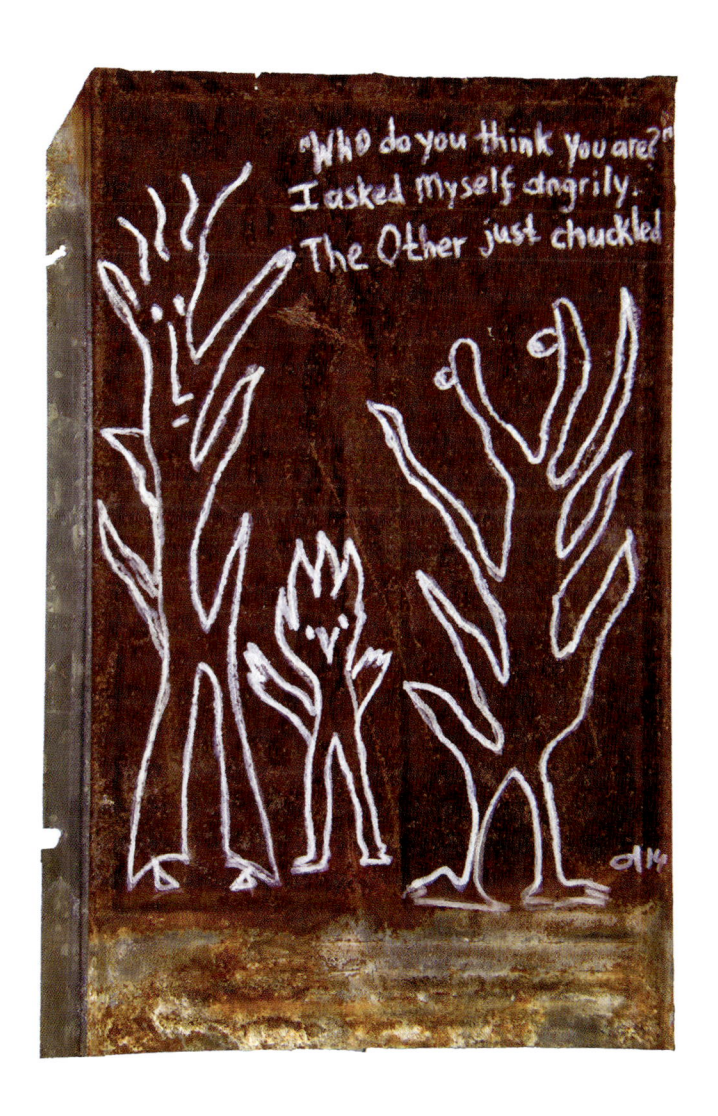

Can I return myself to the manufacturer and ask to be exchanged?

Unhappiness steals time.

I am not unreasonable – I am just incompatible.

❂

Life is a cemetery of memories.
Facebook provided some resurrection services.

❂

Several days in a row, waking up with a terrible migraine. How humiliating it is to feel so dependent on your body, on its limitations, its weakness.... But the body also grounds us, connects us to nature, injects us with humility. I'm not my body. I'm not my mind, either. I'm somewhere else.

❂

How do you rate your work as a suicide-hotline operator? Talk about responsibility...

230 EXCESS OF BEING

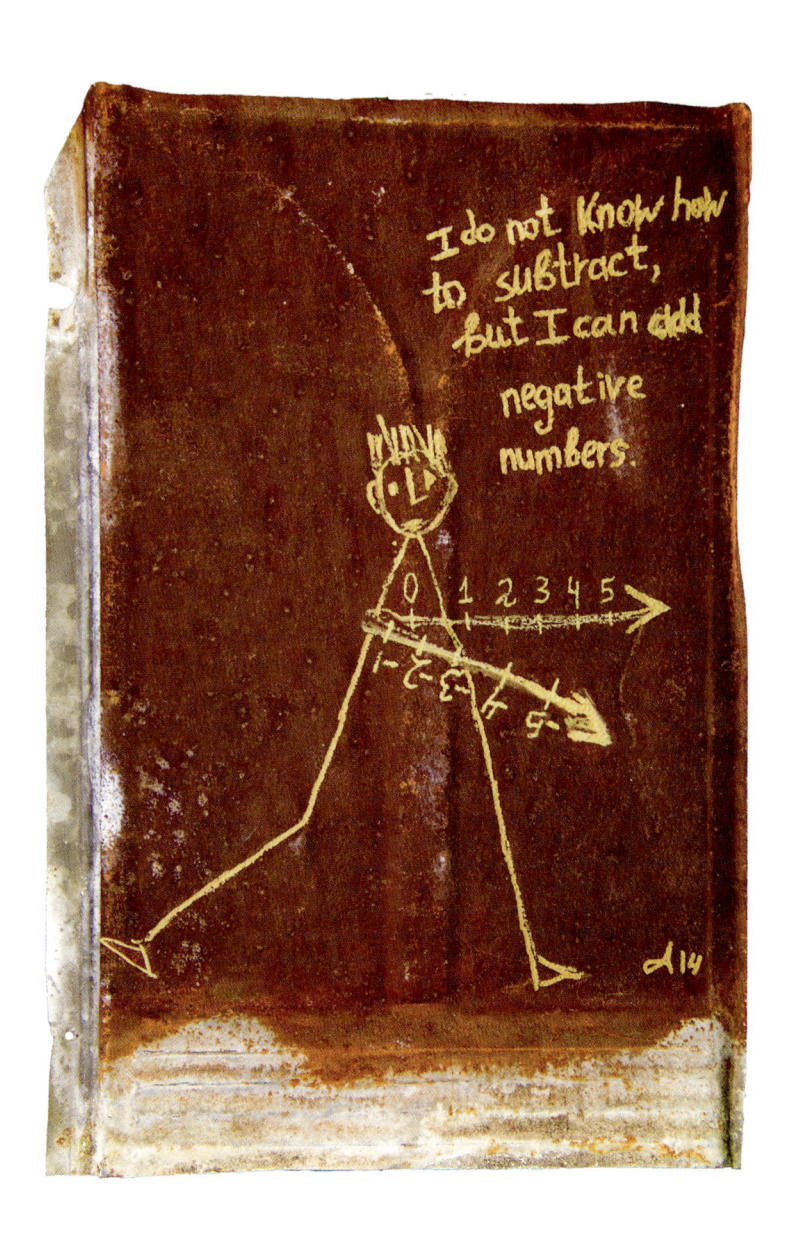

◎

A person who planted a tree will think twice before cutting it down.

◎

I have a tragically flawed relationship with Time. It's a continuous war in which I get tired and wounded, but continue this fight while Time is not even aware of my existence. It is how, probably, a flea feels toward a man. One day a man may accidentally kill this flea without even noticing and end its constant fight against his presumed dominance.

◎

Once upon a time, Time disappeared. People did not notice and kept on winding their clocks.

232 **Excess of Being**

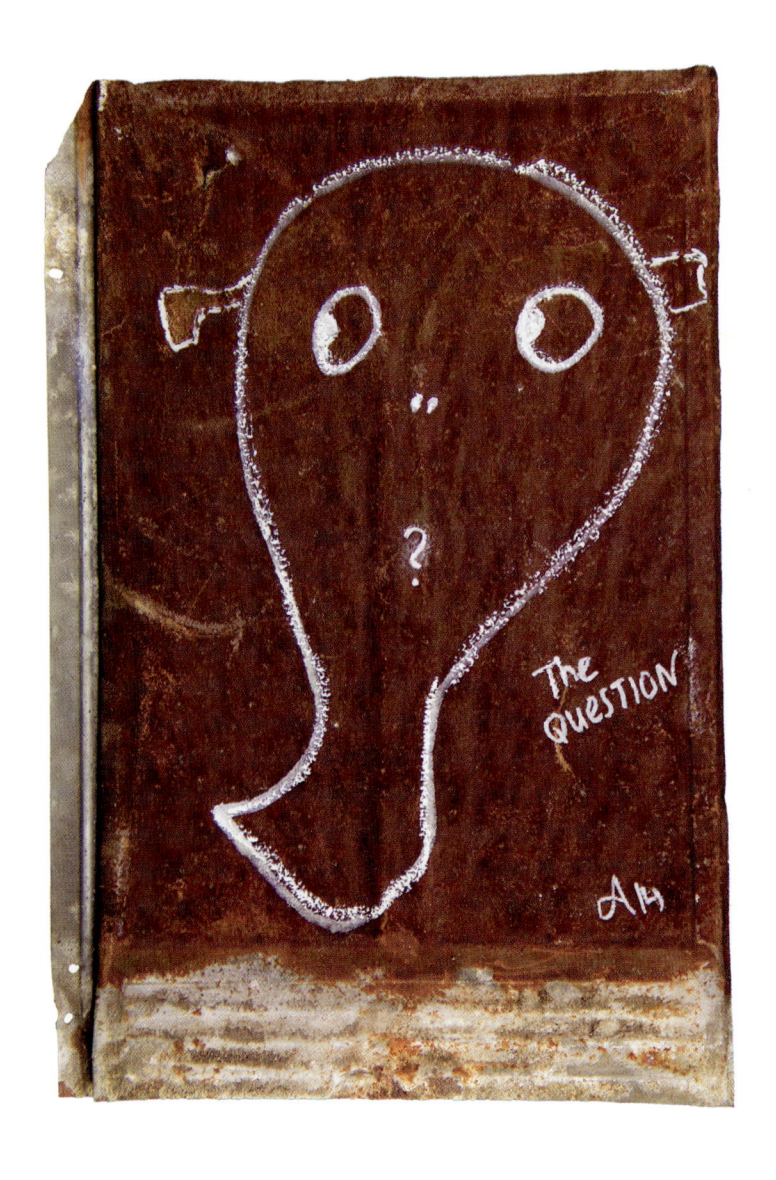

FINDINGS 233

◎

I approve in general but disapprove in particular.

◎

This skeleton is better articulated than its owner ever was.

◎

He developed an obsessive need to create a whirlpool of activity: tweeting, webbing, emailing, sending instant messages, twirling – constantly convincing himself of his own existence.

❦

A midlife crisis occurs when you realize that you are actually living your life, that what you see is what you get, that nothing is going to change because this *is* your life, all molded and designed, and the unimaginable future is indeed imaginable and doesn't look any different from your present. This predictability makes you feel enslaved, so you rebel and make mistakes that complicate and limit your already limited future.

❦

The woman who cleaned my teeth today at the dentist office said: "I'm so jealous of your travels. I never go anywhere. I have no culture. My sister went to France. She said they had such restaurants there… and they put chocolate into everything!" She sincerely believed that culture, like chocolate, can be digested in a restaurant. But what is culture anyway? Maybe she is right and what culture amounts to just melts into a sticky mess. One day you may find yourself staring into the bathroom's mirror and you are old, naked and pathetic, and there is no culture anywhere in sight.

❦

I do not know how to subtract, but I can add negative numbers.

236 Excess of Being

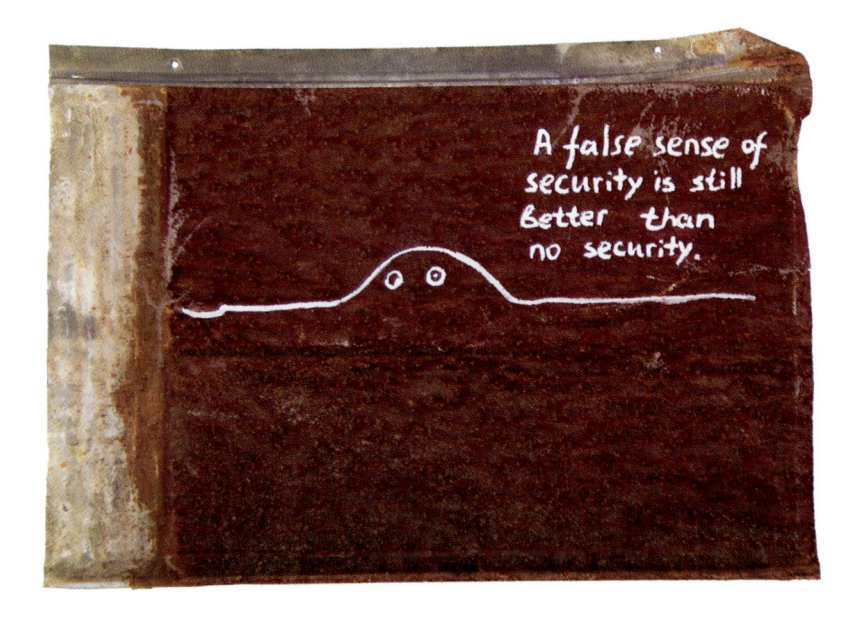

A false sense of security is still better than no security.

❊

I feel crushed by the weight of my personality.

❊

Age is measured by desires.

❊

Wishing well, full of well-wishers.

Key to abundance: Unlock your luck by removing beliefs in your lack.

Can regress be considered progress?

I am so negative – it is positive.

❀

Please take into consideration that I have most inconsiderate surroundings.

❀

Everyone agrees that editing and proofreading written work is necessary. But what about editing your life? Cut, cut, cut everything that steals your time, everything nonessential. These are the weeds that threaten your garden.

❀

Thinking of the future, he is always playing chess with an invisible opponent and his opponent is often winning.

I wish I could erase my worries, but my worries are erasing me.

❦

Don't worry my worries!

❦

False modesty: He proudly parades his sins.

You pay a high percentage on free advice.

A coward is a servant of his fears.
A hero enslaves his fears.

Experience can be the greatest hindrance.

Realized dreams often turn into nightmares.

This is my best behavior at its worst.

"Life is not a prison, life is not a prison, life is not a prison…" (Keep on repeating.)

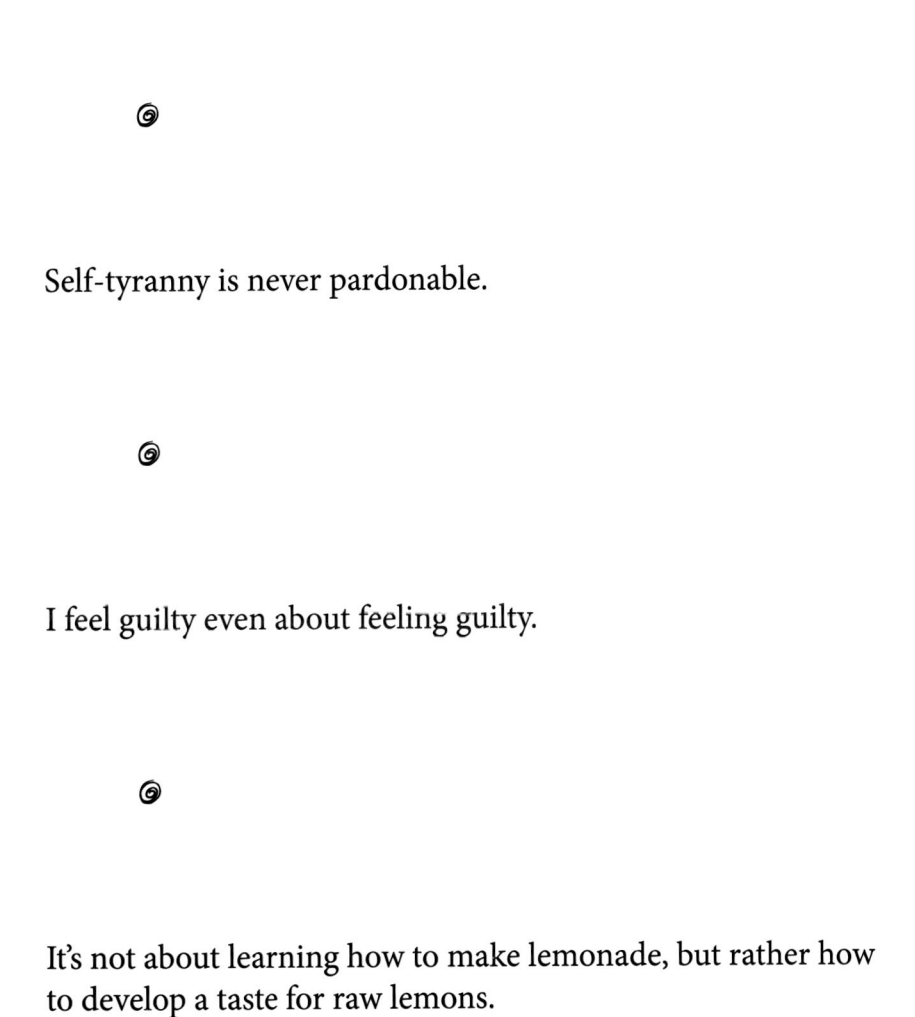

❦

Self-tyranny is never pardonable.

❦

I feel guilty even about feeling guilty.

❦

It's not about learning how to make lemonade, but rather how to develop a taste for raw lemons.

◉

I wish I would be taken care of by invisible gnomes. They would cook and clean, take care of groceries and laundry, write checks and fill out forms. They would also refill my bank account. I would never see them face to face or even be certain of their existence.

◉

I would
if I could
doesn't mean
I can't.

◉

Life passes regardless
of what you think of its passing.

It's ALL TOO much to Bear!
(especially that which is too little)
14

Fragile Solitudes
on wings and vanishing maps of memories

◉

I'm not autistic –
I'm artistic.
Both conditions
spring
from incurable
excess
of being.

◉

Given
enough
time –
all colors
turn
gray.

Life
is a
curable
illness

❂

Even chocolate
tastes bitter
when full of hurt.

❂

It is not possible
to hold a butterfly
without hurting its wings.
Who understands the pain
of a caught insect?

◎

Staying still
is the best
option
when
everything
is spinning.

◎

Time is
gray
in color
and cold
to the touch.

◎

Despair:
When this is over,
you won't even remember.

◎

The present moment
lasts
between two
heartbeats,
yet contains
a lifetime.

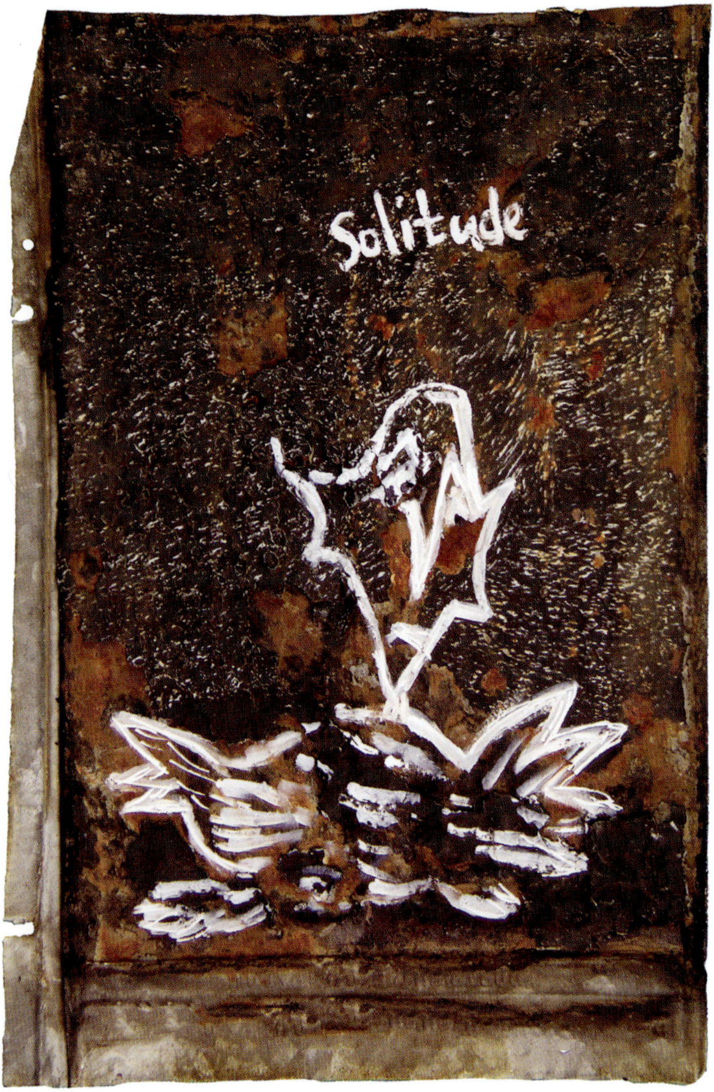
Solitude

❋

My dog
had a nightmare.
I woke him up
gently
with a lie:
"It's all right,
I will never
leave you
alone."

❋

Being a poet
is not a profession,
but a state of mind.

❂

Awakened,
unbearably perfect,
the present moment
lasts.

❂

My hair feels like straw
ever since I cut it
to hurt you,
but hurt myself
instead.

❂

Success
and failure
are one
and the same,
depending
on perspective.

❂

Can
honesty
be
deceiving?

◉

Death,
like life,
is
possessed
by beauty.

◉

The heron was so white,
almost transparent.
I averted my eyes
to avoid staining it
by looking.

FRAGILE SOLITUDES 259

⊚

The only thing
worse than
impatience
is too much
patience.

⊚

I may be a lost cause
but don't you dare
give up on me.

◎

If objects
do not appear
in the mirror,
it doesn't mean
they do not exist.

◎

Grow
ideas
in silence.

◎

Rivers
don't stop
to glance
behind.

◎

This moment
is razor-sharp,
leaving me
bleeding
through
memories.

Fragile Solitudes 263

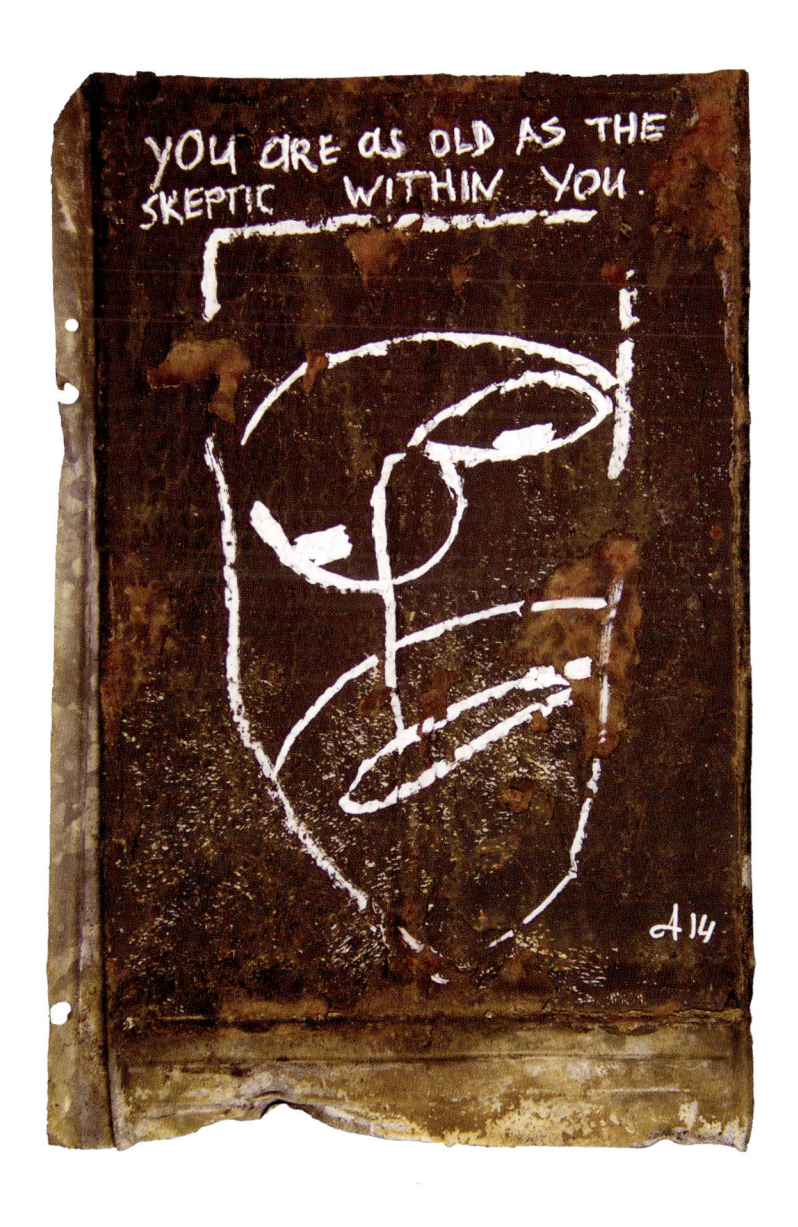

◎

The child I was
didn't survive
adolescence.
It's her death,
the death of a stranger
I lament.

◎

Most memories
are forgotten
more than once.

◎

Young people are unashamed
of big words or concepts;
avoiding them is a sign of maturity;
scorning them is a sign of old age.
You are as old as the skeptic within you.

◎

My solitude was broken
by the intrusion of loneliness.

❦

Dying
too
takes
time.

❦

Sometimes I look
at an old photograph
of myself. I'm five years old,
sitting on top of the trunk
of my father's car,
looking straight ahead
with such heart-wrenching trust
and seriousness….
I hope that I did not
betray you too much, child.
I hope that we are
not too irrevocably apart.

FRAGILE SOLITUDES 267

I stepped aside. my life kept on going without noticing my absence.

❂

Suicide is a forbidden country;
yet, it doesn't require a visa
and its borders are vast and wasteful.

❂

Aging
happens
when growing
stops.

❂

I stepped aside.
My life kept on going
not noticing my absence.

Fragile Solitudes 269

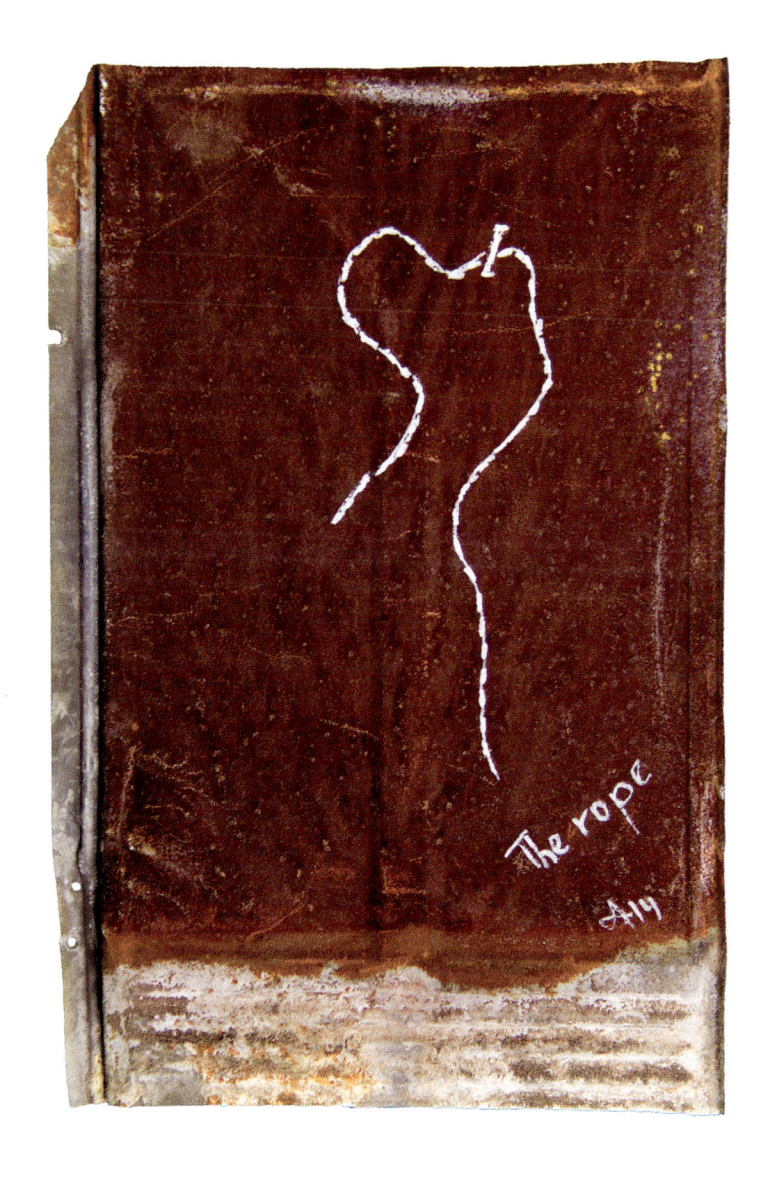

My old address book is an archaeological find:
Flipping its pages, I find extinct specimens,
whose origins I no longer recall.

I live
on the threshold
between now and never.

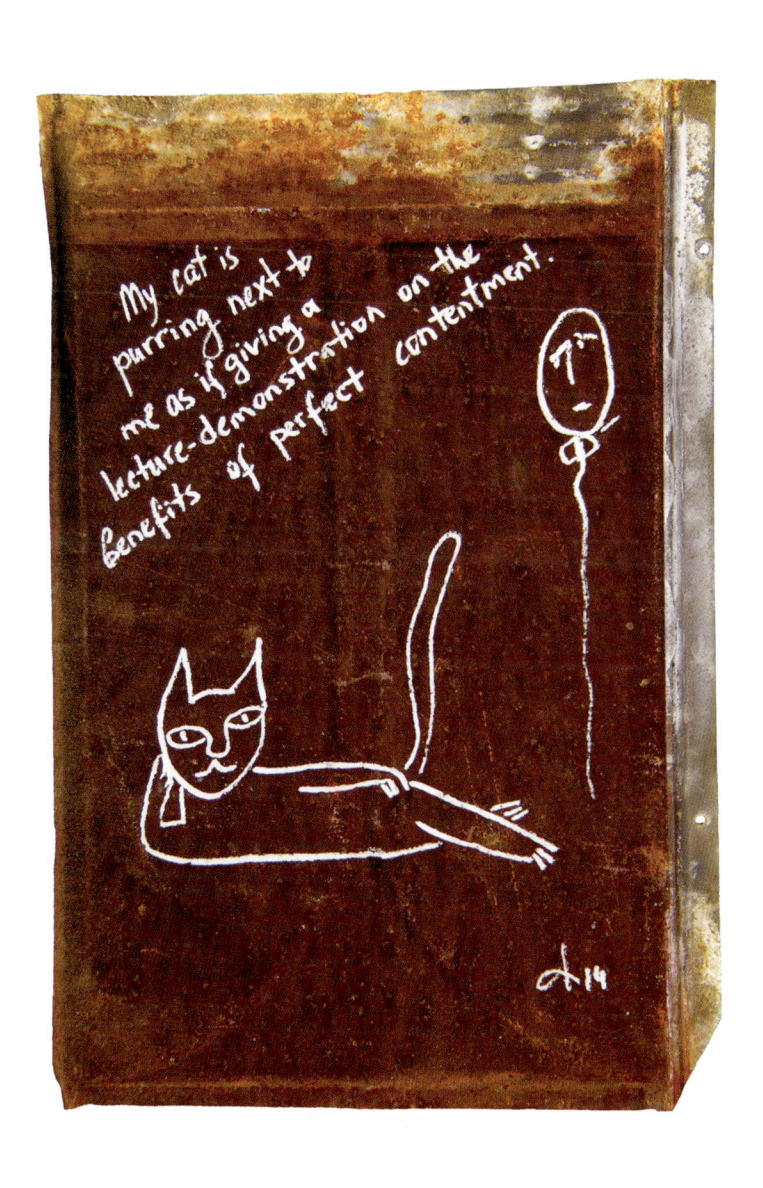

My cat is purring next to me as if giving a lecture-demonstration on the benefits of perfect contentment.

※

All dreams
end up
the same.

※

Shattered future:
I'm looking through the rubble
searching for broken pieces
of future memories.

◉

Graveyards of wishes:
Entire wish lists
like armies of fallen soldiers.

◉

What cruelty is born
from violated
shyness!

274 Excess of Being

◎

My cat is purring next to me
as if giving a lecture-demonstration
on the benefits of perfect contentment.

◎

Conflict occurs
when two pasts step
on the toes of the present.

◉

What is "now"?
The moment I am writing this
or the moment you are reading it?

◉

Today
would have been
more bearable
if behind it
didn't stand
tomorrow.

◉

The maps of memory
change daily.
One more country
vanished today.

Rivers don't stop to glance behind

◎

Cabinet of curiosities:
 – collections of fears,
 – hopes,
 – anxieties,
 – worries,
 – aspirations,
 – desires,
 – wish lists,
 – faded memories,
 – forgotten places,
 – lost pets,
 – imaginary voices.

◎

Life
is a curable
illness.

Fragile Solitudes 279

Accidentals
on relationships and other misunderstandings

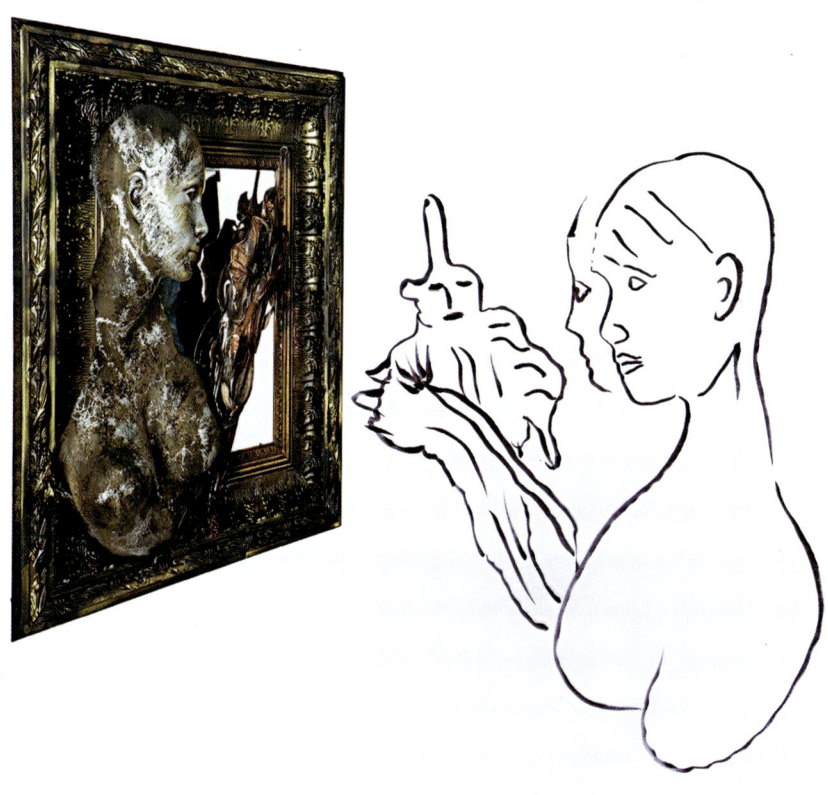

❂

Your presence requires too much of my solitude to balance it.

❂

My desires are undesirable.

❂

Good experiences are built upon accumulated innocence; bad experiences – upon swelled-up skepticism.

◎

If you have a ridiculous situation, don't try to fix it; instead, add an even greater element of absurdity.

◎

He was so positive that I had no choice but to become increasingly negative, for the sake of equilibrium.

◎

I am giving up on my misgivings.

◎

He is erectional.

◎

Marrying your first love has one disadvantage: You never know if you are extraordinarily lucky or if you don't know any better.

◎

Embarrassed to a shameless degree, I'm too hopeful about strangers and too doubtful about friends.

◎

Sex: ransom for the hostages of anatomy.

◎

Love is all you need, but it is not enough.

◎

I rarely miss a person, but often – the idea of a person.

◎

Shall I dilute myself even further or am I already digestible?

◎

Everything has one side
and another side.
And often it's the other one
that matters.

◎

I'm revisiting my old demons. How small and trivial they have become....

288 Excess of Being

◎

Let's not mingle our limitations together – your limitations are all your own.

◎

You are alone, always alone. If you can't accept this – you're not ready for a relationship.

◎

My patience is explosive!

Not having sex is no excuse for having sex.

His need for her approval was so intense that he'd become defensive even at the mere thought of the possible lack of appreciation.

We may be in this together,
but our side effects differ.

◎

Premature election
leads to ejection.

◎

He was so much in love – he never noticed the object of his infatuation.

◎

The Little Mermaid managed to get rid of her tail and learn to walk. The only thing that she could never change was her fishy smell. That's why the prince rejected her. Poor, poor Little Mermaid.

◎

Even though the end result may be the same, there is a difference between undressing and being undressed.

◎

Chronos ate his children; he is still eating them. We are his children.

◎

God gives us a family so that we can do our work.
The Devil gives us a family to prevent it.

Positive thinking: Weakness is strength in disguise.
Negative thinking: Strength is weakness in disguise.

I resist
my impulse
to resist.

The ability to forgive is a measurement of love.
The more we love – the more we are capable of forgiveness.

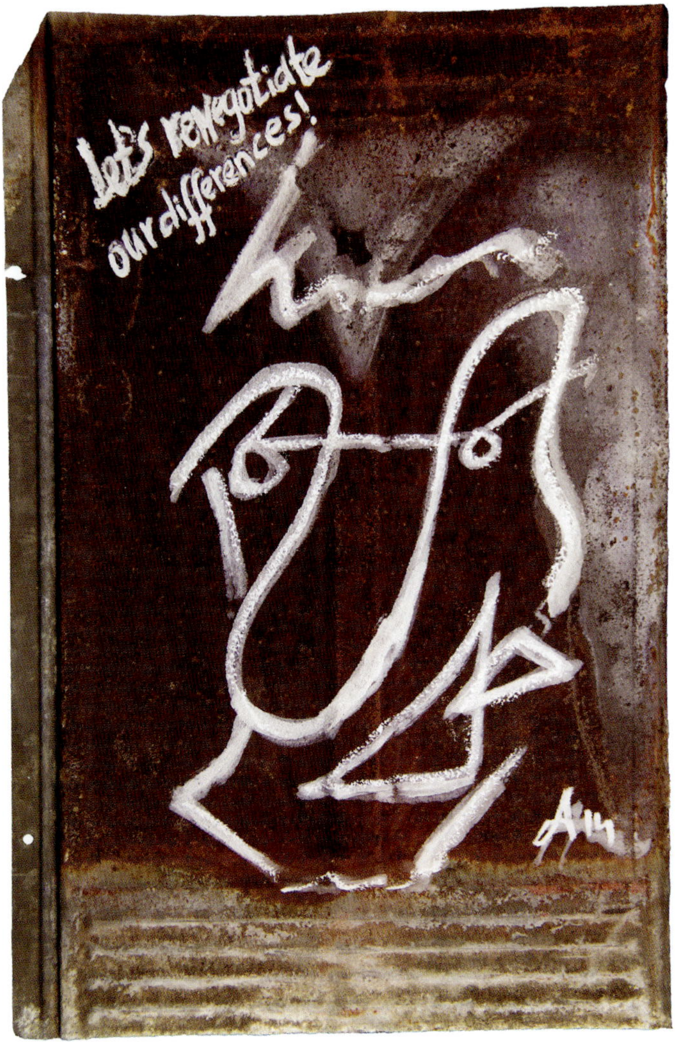
Let's renegotiate
our differences!

❂

Divorce is a temporary insanity. Be careful – it is also contagious.

❂

Lust is the body's revenge for the soul's immortality.

❂

He wears his face like a death mask.

◎

Texting can be dangerous *not only* when driving.

◎

When my first boyfriend mentioned the word "sex," I was offended. "Why are you talking to me about sex? I thought you loved me!"

◎

Can I just apologize for everything in advance, so that when the time comes – you are not offended?

❂

The desires to be loved and to be left alone are not mutually exclusive.

❂

Gay men are much better than straight men. They are more intelligent, more sensitive, more fun, more stylish, more creative, better friends, better listeners....
Too bad they are gay.

❂

Going out with a gay man is like having a delicious appetizer for dinner instead of a heavy meal.

Reaching without reaching – the definition of romanticism.

He was proud of his humility, and failed to sense this hypocrisy.

It's not about the glass being half-empty or half-full. It's about who gets to drink it.

◎

It's not what we talk about. It's what we *don't* talk about that defines our relationship.

◎

Everything in moderation? But what if I'm in the mood for overflowing exuberant generosity of the spirit?

◎

It is despair that I can't contain. Happiness doesn't give me much trouble.

300 Excess of Being

❦

Even a porcupine needs a hug sometimes.

❦

I wish to be loved unconditionally. This is my condition.

❦

I don't care about what is humanly possible;
I want only what is humanly impossible.

◎

Flying is easy enough. It's when I have to crawl that the bleeding starts.

◎

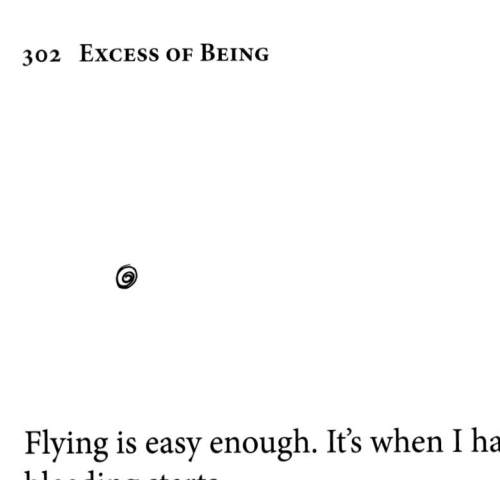

She's been imprisoned by her good taste and is serving a life sentence.

◎

Sex contains "ex" for a reason.

❧

Unspoken words are harassing the silence.

❧

You've successfully expanded the scale of my disappointments.

❧

Forgive me. Especially if you can't.

❊

I puncture my heart with punctuation.

❊

I am not in the mood to be in the mood.

❊

Some days I am dangerous to be next to. Some days I am even dangerous to be away from. Some days even my name in your address book hurts.

Slow down: You are entering erogenius zones.

Unresolved promises poison the heart.

She harvests guilt and releases it at strategic moments.

Excess of Being

FLYING IS EASY ENOUGH.
It's when I have to crawl that the bleeding starts.

❂

I miss myself,
but the feeling
is not mutual.

❂

It kills me that it doesn't kill you.

❂

Sex is anatomy in motion.

◉

You don't need to hear the song
to know that it is sounding.

◉

We notice very little
how little we notice.

◉

Choose your guilt wisely.

◎

He was planning his escape even before he planned his conquest.

◎

Women are the sacrificial version of men.

◎

Making music is not that different from making love: Is your priority to give or to receive?

My nervous system has lost its system, leaving only the exposed nerves.

I wish I could give you all I have and more, but I can only give you more.

Sensuality is sophisticated sexuality.

Accidentals 311

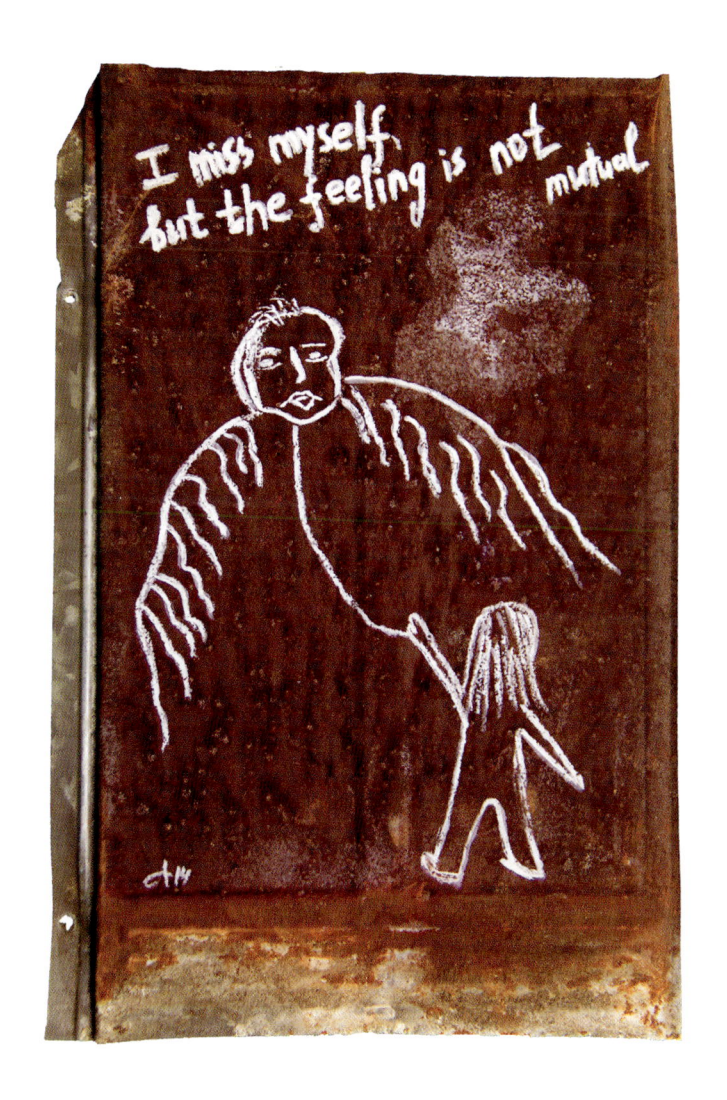

◎

Good excuses are based on solid reasoning. Unfortunately, there is no such thing as a good excuse.

◎

Despair is the certainty of loss.

◎

There is something vaguely humiliating about being a wife. What a weird concept....

Desire comes before fulfillment. If something is missing in your life – check the intensity of your desire for it.

A man's anatomy can be so… exaggerated.

My X-rays are X-rated.

◎

I went to get a pedicure. The woman (pedicurist) commented that she was going to the gym afterward. "How often do you exercise?" I asked. "Every day," she answered. "I wish I could be as disciplined as you," I complimented her. "But you don't need to," she objected. "You're already married!"

◎

May I excuse myself from excusing myself?

◎

To love is not a verb but a state of being. One never "makes" love. If you have to "make" it, that means it is not yet there; it does not exist. There is no such thing as a figure of speech.

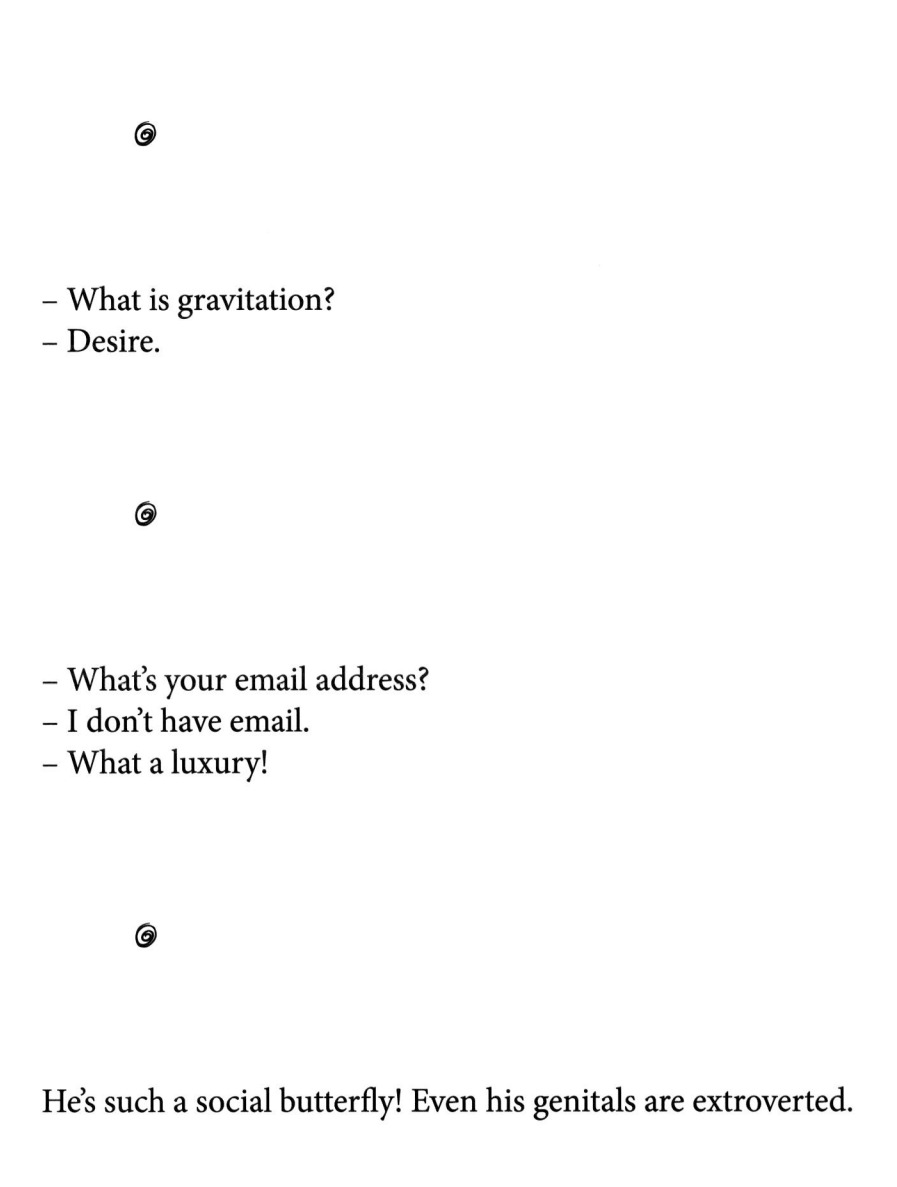

❂

– What is gravitation?
– Desire.

❂

– What's your email address?
– I don't have email.
– What a luxury!

❂

He's such a social butterfly! Even his genitals are extroverted.

316 Excess of Being

❂

I feel discouraged by your encouragement.

❂

I can't take it anymore. Not even for granted.

❂

Just for the record: I'm not gay – I'm sad.

I'm not indifferent – I'm different.

An unforeseen foresight can be frightening.

Sorry, I didn't mean for my bleakness to over-shine your brightness.

You don't need to be so directly indirect with me.

Sex: desirable frictions inevitably leading to undesirable frictions.

Successful marriage means creating enough space for the survival of two solitudes.

◉

Sex at its best dissolves the ego into pure nothingness. So is inspiration, that elusive moment of being 'in the zone,' when you step outside of time into everlasting ever-presence, just to return some moments later, feeling a mix of elation and defeat.

◉

Don't share your limitations with your loved ones or you may risk passing them on.

◉

I need a prescription of carefully measured solitude. Instead, I'm getting overdoses of loneliness.

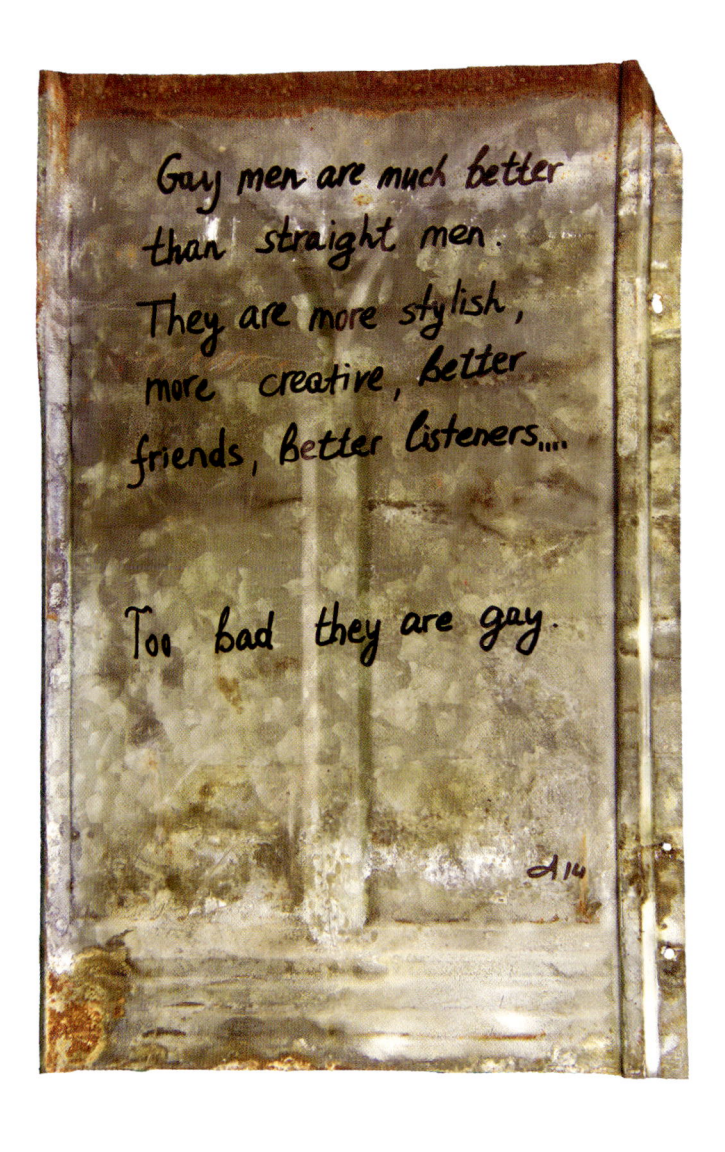

Gay men are much better than straight men. They are more stylish, more creative, better friends, better listeners....

Too bad they are gay.

◉

No, this is not lust – I'm just testing if we are still alive.

◉

He wanted to preserve himself to the point of self-destruction.

◉

The man on the moon
is writing a love letter
but can't recall
the name of his beloved.
He's in exile
for the crimes long forgotten.
Time stands still
for the man on the moon.

❊

No, I don't know what you mean and I suspect you don't know either – that's why you are asking if I know what you mean. No, I'm not mean. Not at all.

❊

Too many responsibilities hurt response abilities.

❊

Accessories make access complicated.

◉

Every time I hear Ravel's *La Valse*, I get aroused. Oh, the powers of seduction from beyond the grave.

◉

Flirting makes me uncomfortable: I'm not good at making promises I will not fulfill.

◉

"You know, boys pee differently than girls," my nanny told me before taking me to kindergarten for the first time. "How do they do it?" I asked. My nanny explained. I laughed and laughed and laughed…. This whole boy thing seemed so redundant.

◉

I feel unloved by myself.

◉

S. felt miserable about his present because he was so disappointed about his future.

◉

Stay away from those who claim to wish you well. Well-wishers are rarely well-doers.

Your exaggeration is understatement.

❂

The present moment alters not only the future but the past. A couple going through a nasty divorce rarely remembers their tender love for each other.

❂

Can in-laws be outlaws?

❦

Practice helps. By creating a woman, God fixed his Op. 1 issues.

❦

Possible side effects:
- irritations
- allergies
- swellings
- venereal diseases
- children.

❦

First I lost my temper, then my temper lost me.

328 Excess of Being

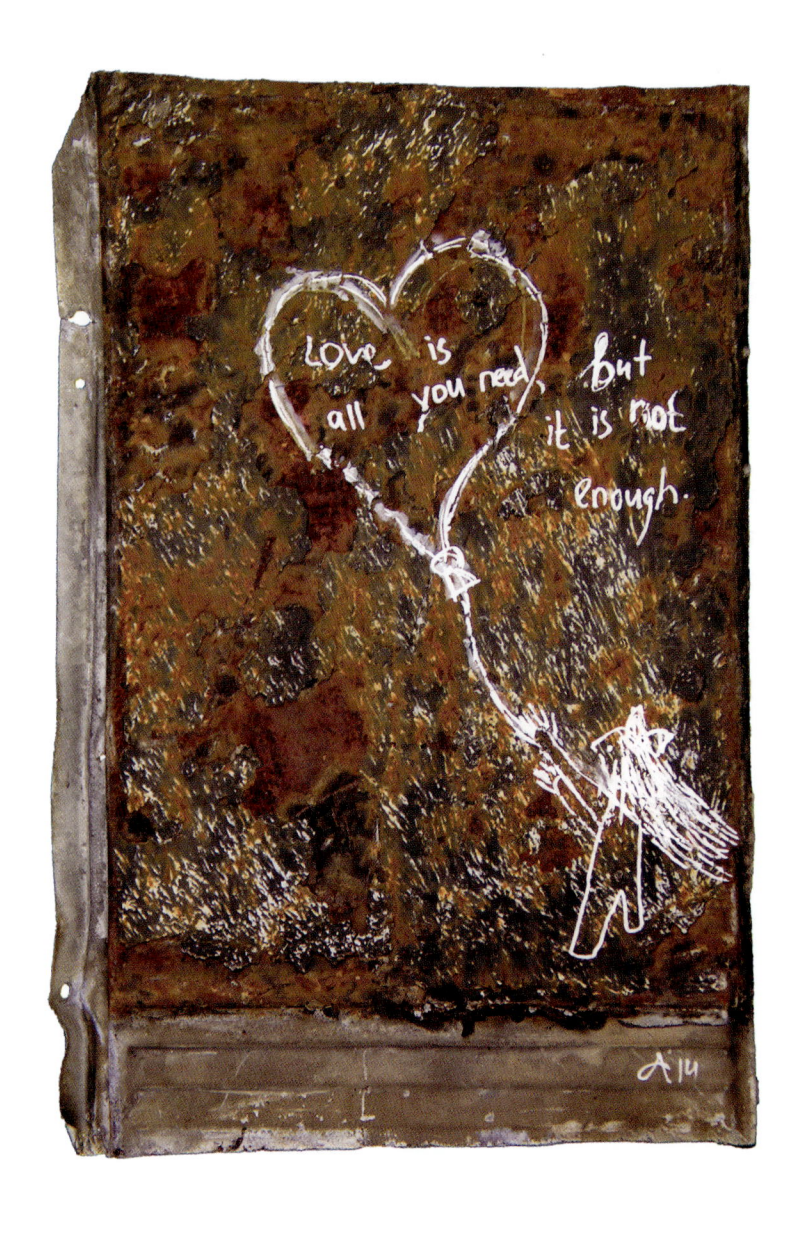

◉

"You play like a man," one famous pianist complimented me backstage after our joint performance in a gala concert. He meant this as the highest compliment. And he would have been stunned if someone pointed out how condescendingly chauvinistic his remark was. I've heard this so many times: "You play like a man; you write like a man; you think like a man," even "you shake hands like a man." Always meant as a compliment, like a pat on the shoulder, a sign of approval.... I heard this phrase from both men and women, and certainly I would take offense if someone would say, "You play like a woman." "Thank you," I answered to the famous pianist. "You play like a man, too," and watched with some satisfaction a shadow of confusion momentarily crossing his face.

◉

Can we trade our inconsistencies?

Where did the word 'deflowering' originate? Virgin girls aren't flowers. By plucking a flower, we are killing it. So, by the same logic, deflowering a virgin has murderous overtones. There is also a sense of loss. "She lost her virginity," we say, although virginity is not something that can be reclaimed in the lost-and-found. There is a hint of self-gratification of the hunter: The flower is plucked and sacrificed for enjoyment.

'Making love' is an even worse expression. How can one 'make' love? The verb 'make' is senseless. Loving is a state of being, a state of awareness. The verb, the action, is signified by another noun – sex.

Things don't get any better there. The expression 'to have sex' is just as flawed. If you can 'have' sex, you must be able to 'give' sex. The linguistic jungle reflects our confusion of the sexual nature of human experience and its moral and religious conditioning.

◎

My reflections are averting eyes.

◎

Warning: Treat me gently – I am perishable.

◎

We have subscribed to different versions of time.

◉

Let's renegotiate our differences!

◉

We should be treating each other much gentler. After all, from birth we are terminally ill.

◉

I am not making a face, this *is* my face.

Accidentals 333

◉

N.'s problem was that he could never finish anything he started. Even his failures were incomplete.

◉

Without desire nothing is possible.

Accidentals 335

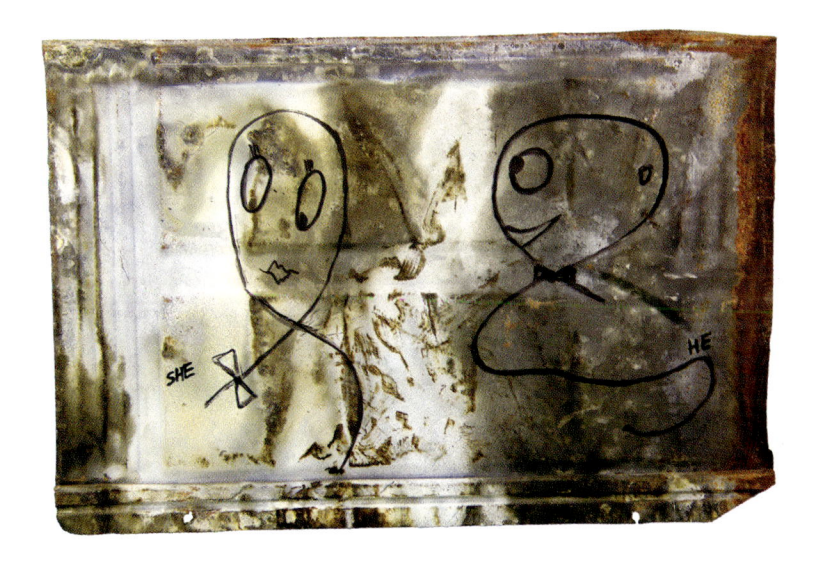

ETERNiday
on angels, demons and wannabes

Saw an ad on eBay: "Selling my soul, no reserve, starting at $1." Felt tempted to place a bid. One never knows what might prove useful in the future.

I wished on a falling star for a graceful falling.

You're stepping on my metaphysical toes.

Enchantment is easy; sustaining enchantment requires stamina.

When placed in front of a bright light, I become a shady character.

He who condemns in the name of God is on the Devil's payroll.

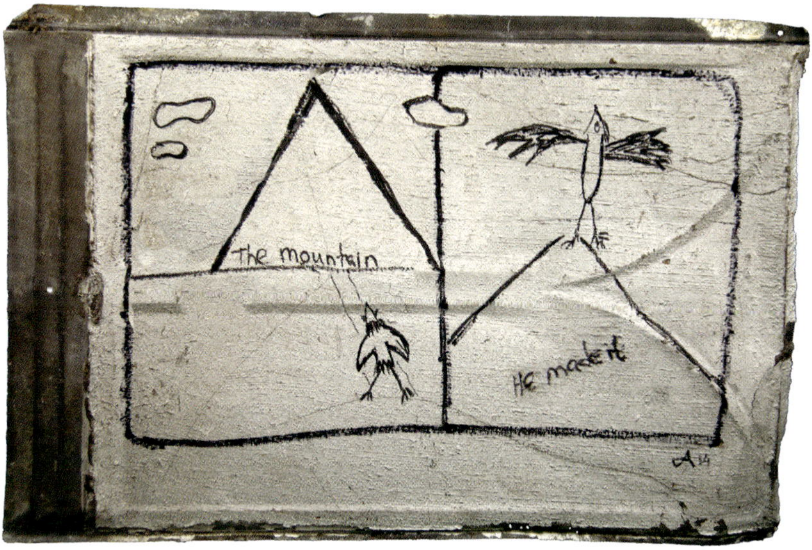
The mountain
HE made it

IF YOU BELIEVE IN THE
power of MAGIC—
YOU HAVE magical
powers.
A!14

◎

Your act of giving doesn't mean that the other is receiving.

◎

It's Mercury retrograde again? What a relief! Finally, I can blame everything on the stars.

◎

My soul has requests; my body has priorities. Both disregard me as an irrelevant independent third party.

He spent many years trying to reach perfect thoughtlessness. Divine enlightenment and complete stupor have more in common than meet the eye.

If you can't make fun of your religion, it's not worth being serious about it.

All of my friends are imaginary, even the real ones.

Some people are angels; others are testers. Angels protect you; testers challenge you. And then there is your family, your loved ones who manage to be angels and testers at the same time, and drive you to insanity.

I will solve all of these issues by reincarnating.

The strong urge to be next to those one loves is in conflict with the artist's need to be away from those he loves.

346 Excess of Being

Dear Lord, protect me from myself so that I can protect you from your followers.

Can't see anything: My enlightenment is blinding.

Calling on all gargoyles to protect my solitude!

❂

Jesus also prayed to God and it ended badly.

❂

I don't need a rabbit to fall into a deep hole.

❂

How many heavens does it take to turn life on Earth to hell?

❂

To the Demon of Fear: "No, I don't think you're right. I don't think you're wrong. I don't think you *are*."

❂

Feed it with your blood and it will become unstoppable.

❂

Each religion is cruel in its own way, but some are crueler than others.

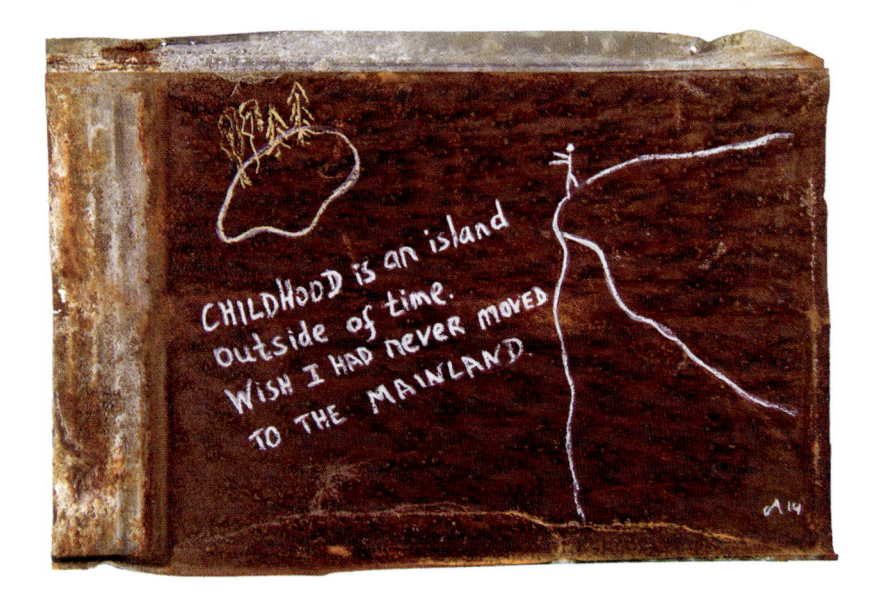

CHILDHOOD is an island outside of time. WISH I HAD NEVER MOVED TO THE MAINLAND.

◉

Unkept promises clutter the soul.

◉

Expanding one's horizons does not necessarily lead to greater depth.

◉

We are always so concerned about hurting religious feelings, but what about hurting feelings of nonbelievers? Isn't it the other way around, and the atheists are much more vulnerable since the believers already have their faith to lean upon?

◉

Bitterness burns.
Into the emptiness
darkness crawls.

◉

Modern archeology: Time buries itself alive.

◉

I gravitate toward levitation.

Power is quiet; weakness is loud.
Power is calm; weakness is restless.
Power doesn't advertise; weakness is a cheerleader.
Power gravitates toward less; weakness wants more.
Power is peace; weakness is a constant challenge.
Power doesn't need approval; weakness seeks appreciation.
Power thinks in centuries; weakness is always busy.
Power is self-contained; weakness needs company.
Power sees what's within; weakness seeks bright surfaces.
Power is somber; weakness is enthusiastic.
Power is inspiring; weakness seeks inspiration.
Power doesn't need power; weakness lusts for influence.
Power is not vain; weakness is fueled by competitiveness.
Power dreams big; weakness is skeptical.
Power is generous; weakness is defensive.
Power carries certainty; weakness needs the next great cause to live for.
Most people confuse one for the other. Be powerful.

With enough time, all belief systems become mythology.

Meetings – building new vessels for the same emptiness.

Hellish advertisement:
"Real estate in Hell is getting very valuable. Location is everything. There are whole towns filled with celebrities. Reserve your spot early or you might end up in the suburbs with religious fanatics."
"What about Heaven?"
"Sorry, but Heaven is completely booked in advance by victimized infidels."

◎

Don't blame the darkness for the shadows. They are caused by light.

◎

I floated in the ocean looking up into the setting sun. The moment was so insanely perfect that the thought crossed my mind that I might have died. Then I had a cramp in my leg and was relieved to realize I am still alive.

◎

The proximity of a pixie can be seen in pixels.

A morning prayer required for an Orthodox male: "Blessed are you, Lord our God, ruler of the universe, who has not created me a woman." As if during the night the ultimate nightmare could have happened and his gender might have been inexplicably altered. The morning is a rebirth and with great relief he finds his sex unchanged and thanks the Almighty for sparing him yet again. What an achievement on God's part! What self-control! If I were God, I'd not be able to restrain myself and for at least one day a year would switch all males into females. See how they fare. See if they can survive that single day. What would happen to their pride, their relationships, beliefs? How many would remain faithful through this ordeal? Women can also switch sexuality for one day. Somehow I don't think this would be too problematic.

My shield is broken. Angelic repair store, anyone?

If I run
out of time,
I shall just
quantum jump.
Hoop-la,
ooh-la-la,
oy vey!

Internal life leads to eternal life.

There is a big difference between tolerance and acceptance. Mosquitoes can be tolerated.

The body doesn't lie. It just doesn't know the truth.

Eterniday 359

Every day a new Icarus kills himself.

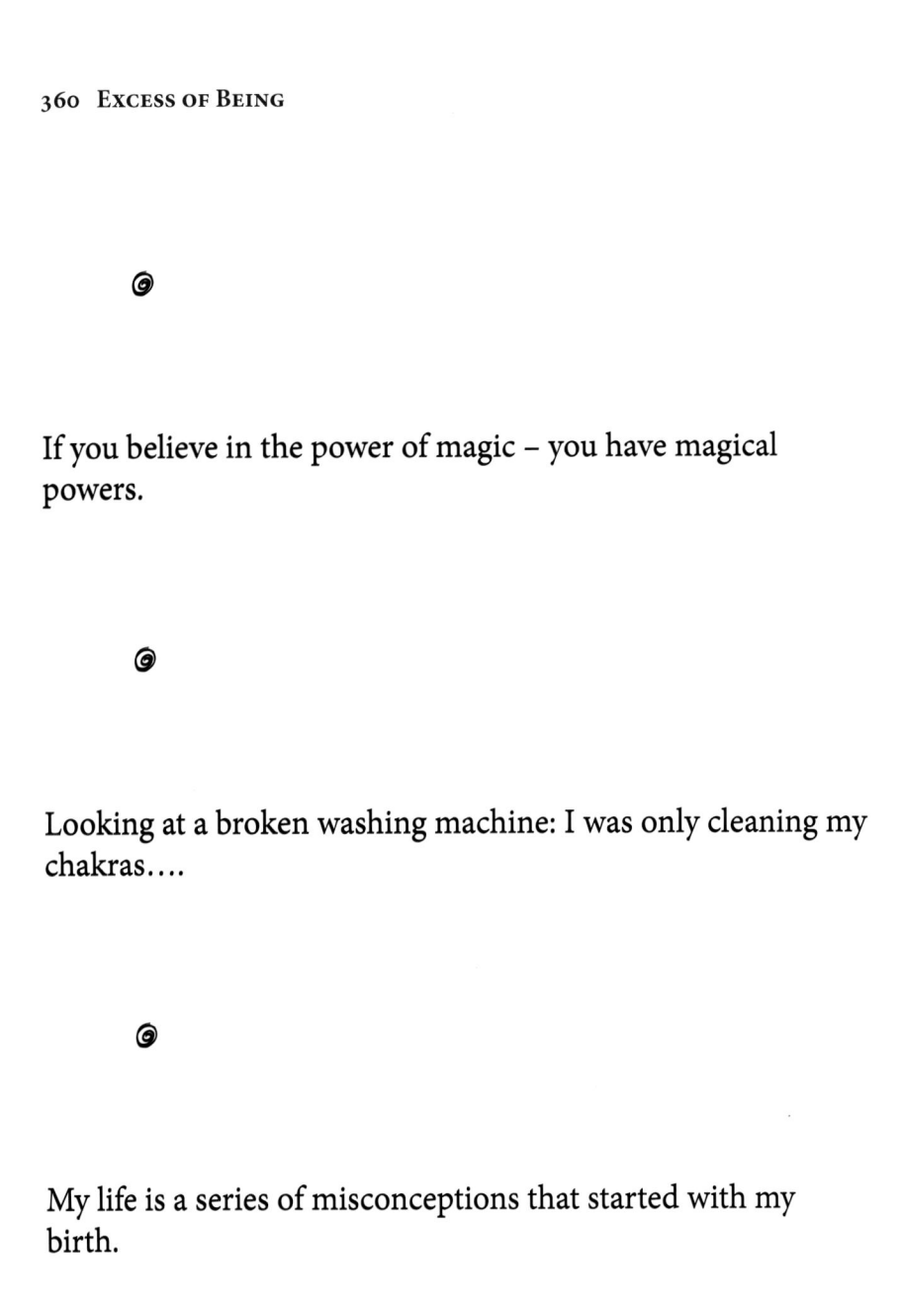

If you believe in the power of magic – you have magical powers.

◎

Looking at a broken washing machine: I was only cleaning my chakras....

◎

My life is a series of misconceptions that started with my birth.

◉

At first, I didn't believe in the existence of Time, but Time always believed in me.

◉

Childhood is an island outside of time. Wish I had never moved to the mainland.

◉

I am nine. My mother is taking me to the dentist. "Yes, it will hurt," she confirms my worst fears. "But it's better to take out this tooth sooner than later. Otherwise it will hurt even more." "This is like dying, then," I reply. "Wouldn't it be better for me to die now, since I will have to die at some point anyway?" "You have a long life ahead." "You mean it will hurt a lot? And for a long time? And then I die anyway?" My mom grows quiet and then says, "It's just a tooth."

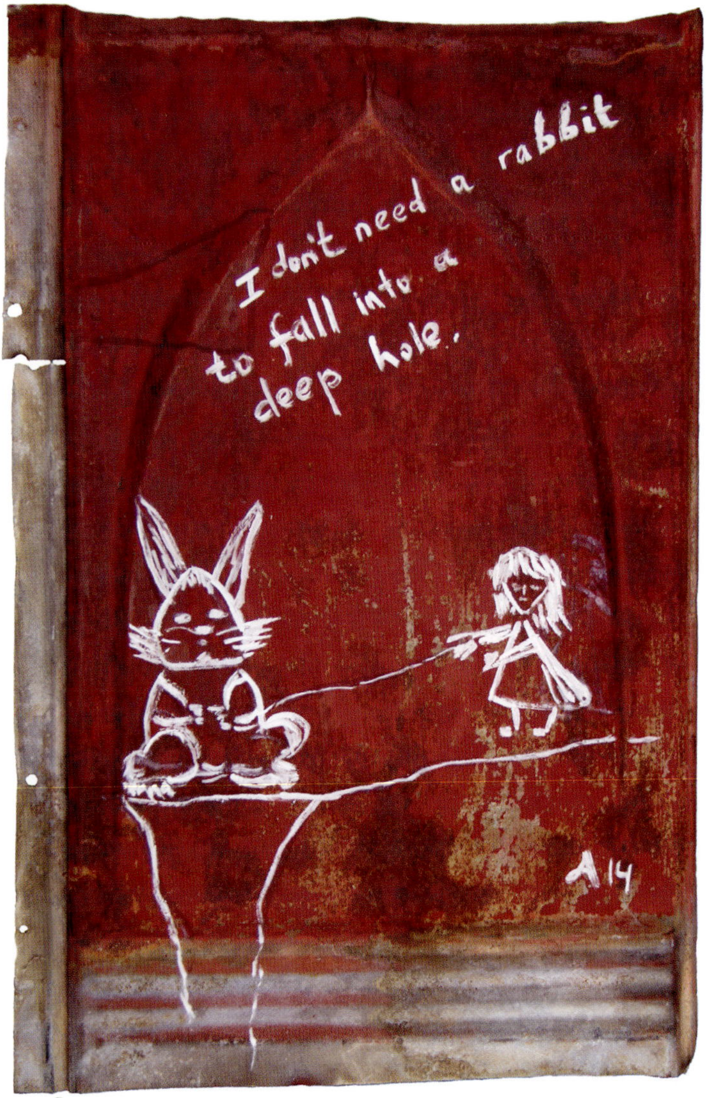
I don't need a rabbit
to fall into a
deep hole.
A 14

The ghosts are better than the living. At least they do not add to pollution. Or do they?

Ecstasy, orgasm, inspiration and revelation all have something in common: letting go of one's ego, letting go of self-awareness; dissolving, if only for a few blissful moments, into something greater than oneself; feeling one with the infinite continuum, where time and space become one, where everything is interconnected. The memory fades as soon as it's over, as soon as time and space break their embrace and focus on the present moment. You are back in your imperfect vessel, dazed and amazed, but already forgetting, because experiencing the duality of finite and infinite is exhausting and confusing, and because life requires you to go on. That's what life does – it always goes on. Until it doesn't.

We know exactly what our afterlife is. After all, we are living it.

❋

In order to understand the circle, you need to break free from the square.

❋

Prophets must be very insecure creatures if they require such violent defending by their followers.

◎

I'm more than all I am.

◎

I'm one with my song, yet my song is infinitely better than I am.

◎

Demons feed on fears. Angels feed on hopes.
The pendulum swings between fears and hopes until they become indistinguishable.

Dying is contagious. It may become a way of life.

Don't blame me for your enlightenment – I'm still in the dark.

Cows are (also) chosen before being slaughtered.

◎

I have my demons; you have yours. Do you want to swap without looking?

◎

Don't let a random fortune teller predict your future. She may call it into being.

◎

I'm the optimistic prophet of doom.

368 Excess of Being

◎

Certainty is attractive, but can be just as misleading as insecurity.

◎

Fighting depression is difficult as it fights you on your own ground. It's your enemy – the enemy who wears your face. It speaks with your own voice and you are no longer capable of distinguishing between the two of you.

◎

Broken thoughts are better – their shards reflect the light.

For many, praying is giving advice to God on the best course of action.

I am not an atheist, but prefer an atheist over a religious zealot.

Don't worry about the diet – keep your soul kosher.

◎

The dead are more eager to communicate with the living than vice versa.

◎

Most demons are born from men and gain power from strong emotions: fear, anger, greed, power, lust. If you don't want these demons in your life, don't participate in feeding them.

◎

I have no idea how to live my life, but have a pretty good concept of how to ruin it.

❂

Translation from the Divine to the Human ought to have numerous misunderstandings. And then Babylon with all its linguistic confusion… We are all victims of a ruined vocabulary.

❂

I believe in God, but am weary and wary of God's worshipers.

❂

God and gut sound similar for a good reason – one resides in the other.

◉

In guts I trust.

◉

– God bless you!
– And who are you to command the Almighty?

◉

Being chosen was never a good omen.

◎

As long as anti-Semitism exists, I consider myself Jewish. Not because of the religious beliefs, but because I don't like bullies.

◎

We condemn by naming.

◎

The world of the dead is much closer to the living than we realize.

Looking at a broken washing machine—
I was only cleaning my chakras...

◎

Feelings are colorful thoughts.

◎

You can't sail into the ocean while being safely anchored.

◎

You don't need to travel far to run away from yourself.

He was angry with himself for dying.

Being born is irreversible.

When everyone sings in perfect unison – I need to sing out of tune.

◎

I thought of creating a country for weirdos like myself, where we'd finally have a place to belong. Then I realized I wouldn't be considered enough of a misfit to belong there.

◎

Some days, when feeling particularly lousy, I just give up on myself and immediately feel better.

◎

High morals can be highly immoral.

◎

When my body is my friend – I take it for granted. When my body is my foe – I scream of its betrayals. I certainly wouldn't wish to be in my body's shoes. But if I'm not in my body's shoes – in whose shoes am I?

◎

At school: "Lera, don't be a Jew. Let me copy your homework."

◎

It's not that I am obsessed about leaving a trace, but it would be nice to splash some colors into the gray wastelands of oblivion.

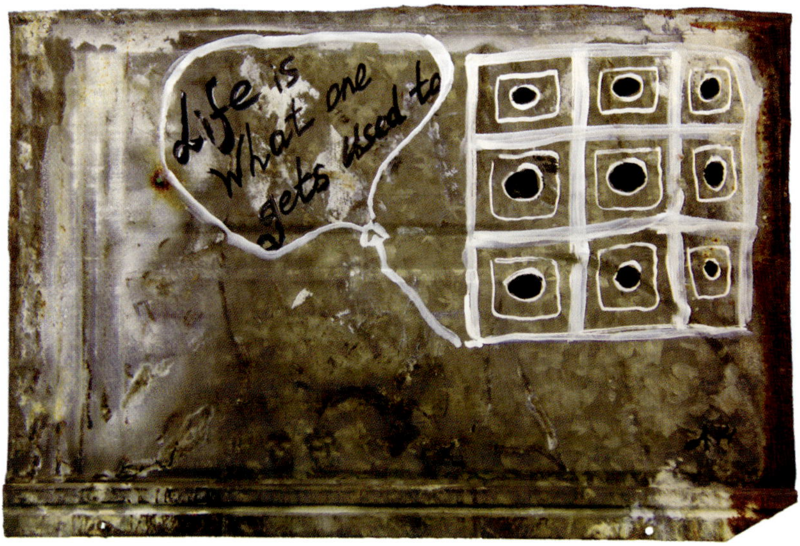
Life is What one gets used to

I have no protection from angels.

Keep your prayers simple – God's patience may be limitless, but better not to test it.

Please don't sell me your god. I'm off the market.

Annual "Christmas market"... How ironic: Wasn't Christ himself enraged when he discovered a market at the temple?

How do you know you have only one shadow?

If you're ready to be burnt for it – it shall be yours.

Suicide is murder, because you're not your own.

Mortality is above morality.

You can count your blessings or you can count your wounds. Either way – time passes.

Overthinking causes stupor.

Best risk-management technique – leave it all to the gods.

Time doesn't change. Time stands still. We change. We pass. We are passing Time.

◎

Angels and demons are like cats and dogs – they fight each other in theory, but, in practice, they share a water dish.

◎

Sometimes being broken
results
in becoming whole.

◎

Take system out of belief
and you are left
with myth.

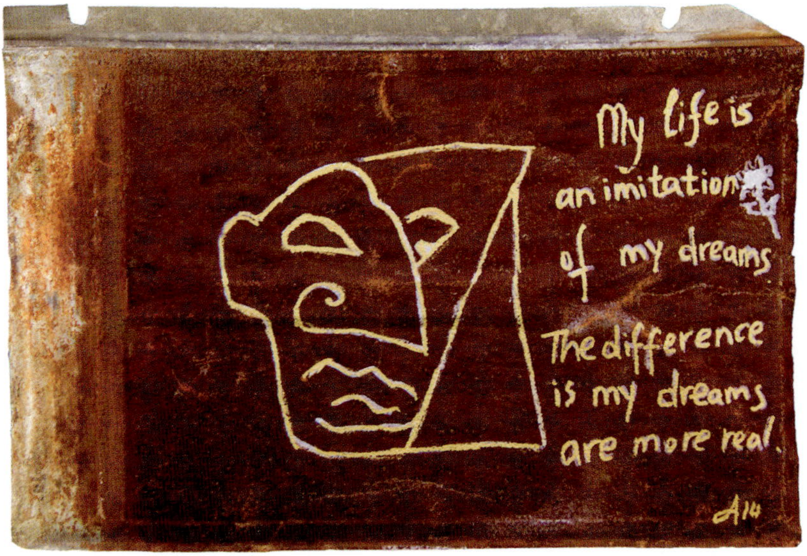
My life is
an imitation
of my dreams
The difference
is my dreams
are more real.
A14

◎

Can you repeat who you are? My reader?
Sorry, I conjured you by mistake.

◎

Actions are inspired by angels.
Reactions – by demons.

◎

Those who claim to know are lost. Let them remain there in that happy or not so happy delirium.

◎

Depression knows no taboos.

◎

Composing "happy" music doesn't lead to a happier life. Talking about God rarely leads to more spirituality. Often the result is opposite of the intent when such correlation is taken literally.

◎

Forgive me, Lord, I accidentally did your work.

You can't calculate risk factors. You can talk to a fortune teller, hire a risk analyst or the most expensive strategic advisor, or just roll the dice: It will amount to the same result. Paying for the projected analysis of possible outcomes doesn't give any more certainty of events to come than practicing magic arts of divination. Either way – you are only feeding the black swans. Enjoy their twisted beauty. Life would be too boring and hopeless with all probabilities calculated.

Nunc ipsum: at the present moment, now. But how long does the present moment last? A minute, a second, a millisecond? Can it even be measured? This intersection of past and future – a blink of perception. Perhaps the present exists only at those moments of self-awareness. Perhaps the observer creates the present by the very act of observation. What makes this elusive "now"?

◎

If you can't face death – you are not truly alive.

◎

Can I return this slice of life back to the kitchen? I think the chef must have been drunk.

◎

Sometimes the ultimate bravery is to get out of bed in the morning, to face yourself and in your loneliest hour to be able to see through the frost on the window.

THE BODY DOESN'T
LIE — it just doesn't
Know the truth.

I'm a hermit who lives on the edge of the world. But the edge of the world is becoming too edgy, and the world keeps on sending various demands by pigeon post. The pigeons are trained to squeak noisily until I grant and answer all requests. It's becoming too noisy and crowded on the edge of the world. I'm a hermit who has nowhere to hide. I'm a hermit in search of a hermitage.

No privacy from God.

After I die – please send me to doggie heaven so I can reunite with my dogs.

◎

Sometimes I feel like crying from the unbearable tenderness toward the present moment: this moment in time; from the inevitability of tomorrow, from the fragility of my state, yet strength of it too, from being still young, healthy and alive, fully alive, from feeling this aliveness and unity with everything around me and from wondering why it is that happiness can feel so sad, and the inadequacy of the words 'happy' and 'sad' and from the futility of all words to express anything essential.

◎

No longer do we know the original language in which words were not reflections of things, but things in themselves, and to call upon something meant to manifest its existence.

Our planet: an aquarium peopled with self-aware holograms who are oblivious that this is a game and unaware of its rules, while the "originals" observe from outside; the former believe they are the latter and that death is real. Poor bastards!

Can notes understand what music is?
Can sounds understand melody?
Can we understand God?

Perfection can be stillborn. Life is messy and imperfect. That's why I like cracked surfaces, ruins, marks of time – they are perfect in their imperfection, in their time-altered beauty.

Sometimes being broken results in becoming WHOLE

◉

Is there a lost-and-found for hopes and dreams?

◉

I need a whole other life not to let this one go to waste.

◉

– What do you do for recreation?
– Angel-wrestling.

◎

From the bird's
point of view
all that matters
are the crumbs
you leave behind.

◎

Edit your actions.
Edit your surroundings.
Edit your thoughts.
Cut, cut, cut.

◎

Mountains do not care
what happens to their climbers.

At night, taking out garbage bags and feeling a quiet despair rising at the impossibility of taking control over life, projects, bills, closets, even over the garbage.... Suddenly a very large—as in a dream—butterfly flew toward the beam of my flashlight. Its wings were so large that I thought it was a bird, at first. There was a sense of urgency, of desire and such beauty that for a moment I forgot everything and just watched this incredible creature as it danced in the air around the beam of light in my hand. Then I remembered why I was there and the familiar despair returned. The butterfly was still there, but the magic spell was broken. I turned around and continued my task. I did not notice when it flew away. And now I wonder if it were indeed a butterfly.... What if it were an angel?

The difference between science and art?
With enough time, scientific theories are proven incomplete or wrong.

◎

My deepest desires have sunk even deeper. Now it would take some risky soul-diving to be able to even glimpse them.

◎

Life can be measured by the grave-markers of desires.

◎

Sometimes the only way to find your way home is to run as far away from it as possible. Sometimes the only way to remember is to forget.

❂

Disenchantment. What a sad word. In D-sharp minor.

❂

What exactly do we remember?
Which version of our lives?

❂

True wisdom doesn't come from thinking. Nor from experience. It is something else altogether.

◎

When you are old, it is easier to be immature.

◎

Wise men say this; wise men say that. They spend their lives saying things, these wise men. And what happened to wise women? They quietly get all the work done.

◎

Wishful thoughts become unwishful thinking.

◎

I carry the whole world on my shoulders. The world seems rather comfortable and is not planning to get off anytime soon. I'm getting weary of this arrangement.

"It's nothing against you, World, but I have other things to do and my wings are getting all wrinkled from being folded for too long and are aching to stretch in flight. Get off now, World, before I use my shrinking magic elixir on you. What is it? No, I'm not falling here from exhaustion, just making it easier for you to get off. Climb down now!"

Sometimes, you need to talk to the world in a stern voice and be rather strict. It's your world, after all, and you are responsible for its whiny, needy behavior. Give it what it needs, instead of what it asks of you – and it will flourish; feed its greedy nature and it will devour your best gifts without even noticing.

◎

Between all or nothing, nothing may be preferable.

Death is much more sustainable than life. Life is temporary; Death is permanent. Life is fragile; Death is unbreakable. Life is fickle; Death is dependable. Life is real; Death does not exist.

Only childlike questions are worthwhile.

As a last resort,
I dreamt of Pegasus
carrying me away
into Forever Beyond.

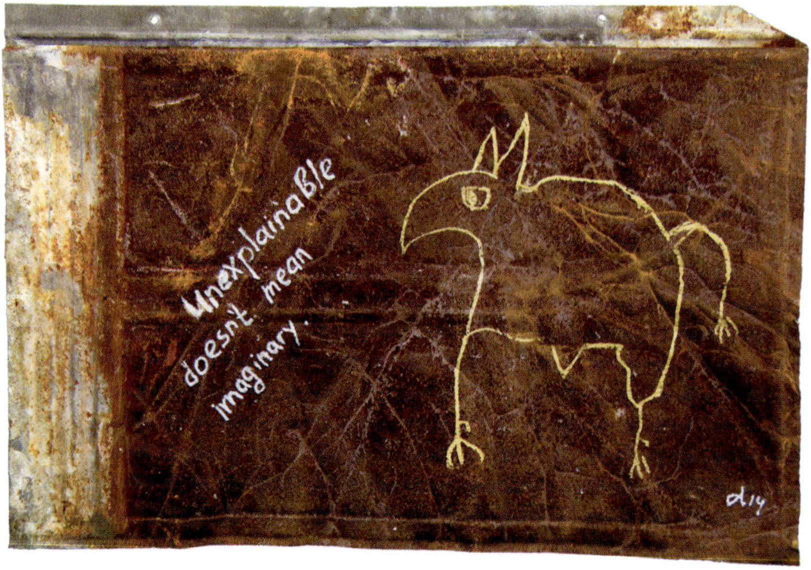
Unexplainable
doesn't mean
imaginary.
d14

◎

After a few days of feasting, the Christmas trees are left on the sidewalks, stripped of their honors, dying: their short lives neither mourned nor remembered. Oh, the slaughter of the innocent, kindergarten of baby trees not meant for this world.... Yearly tree massacre, happening with clockwork inescapability – all while humans are celebrating life and ignoring the tarry tears of the dead.

◎

Homo sapiens? Never met one.

◎

Stay above, always above.... The air might be thinner, but free of pollution.

◎

Don't make an appointment with Disappointment. If you do, you may fall into the routine of follow-up visits until you find yourself living in Disappointment's house of distorted mirrors, instead of your own home.

◎

Exit and Entrance are the same.

◎

I don't subscribe to fatalism, yet some things remain predetermined. Don't you just hate unsolicited deliveries?

Every person, every object, everything around you contains a promise, a possibility. If you can discover and nourish this promise – it turns into a gift.

Heaven: thinking about sleeping with 72 virgins.
Hell: sleeping with 72 virgins.
Hell's hell: the following morning.

The cruelest acts of men are done in the name of God or patriotism.

Who am I? One who thinks these thoughts? What about that deeper part of self that can observe having these thoughts? The deepest "I" is an observer and contemplator, rather than a participant. The composer is, above all, the listener; the deepest urge for being a writer is to be a reader; a man is first a god and only then – human.

To the atheist – so, in which God don't you believe?

Life projection:
Childhood – great promise.
Adolescence – introduction of doubt.
Marriage – end of a fairy tale.
Adulthood – what happens after the end.

If I run out of time, I shall just quantum jump. Hoop-la, ooh-la-la, oy vey!

◎

I appreciate all of your prayers for me, but at the present moment I could use a more tangible investment.

◎

God takes away by giving.

◎

Unexplainable doesn't mean imaginary.

Imaginary doesn't mean nonexistent.

The kingdom of the dead is much vaster than the kingdom of the living. Unless we just keep on recycling.

Prophet Job's eternal lament: God is either cruel or not omnipotent.

Achieving dreams at any cost turns realized dreams into nightmares.

What's the relationship between God and gravity? We don't know anything about gravity except that it exists. We don't know anything about God. And to where do we gravitate?

God and the Devil decided to switch places to see if anyone would notice. No one did.

◉

Religion may be the most brilliant of the Devil's inventions.

◉

All wars are religious wars. Even those that are not.

◉

God doesn't proactively interfere in human affairs; the Devil does. This game of life is unfair: How can one not *not* fall?

414   Excess of Being

◎

Islam exists in a different timeline than Christianity. Only now has it reached its dark ages and the Inquisition period. The clash is not between different theologies and cultures, but between the timelines.

◎

Run away from anyone who wants to teach you an unsolicited life lesson.

◎

Why are terrorists so fascinated with planes? There are many other ways to cause destruction. Planes are irresistibly theatrical – they represent the desire to fly, to be free, to transcend. Attack on flight is castrating the ancient dream, punishing Icarus for rising too close to the sun and daring to flee his dogmatic prison.

Dying is a difficult labor. To shut down all organs – one by one, bodily functions, intricate machinery, so beautifully put together. Dying takes time and can be agonizingly humiliating. Talking to the living from a deathbed requires mental adaptation, a translation of sorts. When I first came to the United States from the Soviet Union, I found it nearly impossible to explain in my letters home what it was like to live in America. It was such an extremely different experience from their everyday reality that I knew my efforts would fail and be misunderstood one way or another. Talking to the living can be a similar experience for a dying man. And there is still that stubborn inner voice that says: "Don't treat me as a corpse-in-waiting. Just talk normally – I'm not dead yet!"

Edit and audit have a lot in common. The question is in the proportion: There is a difference between circumcision and castration.

◎

In a masterpiece, the whole is greater than the sum of its parts. If true, this explains where the soul dwells. Each person is born as a masterpiece. God couldn't make us otherwise. I'm not my body. Certainly, not *only* my body. I'm not my mind: I can observe my thoughts. Then what am I? More importantly – where am I? I wonder if God asks such questions, too.

◎

My life is an imitation of my dreams. The difference is that my dreams are more real.

◎

Hell must be overcrowded by now. May I sublet a room in heaven while the two of you sort things out?

❊

Life is what one gets used to.

❊

Usually it is precisely those we wish to save whom we end up destroying. It is Faust's complex.

❊

Who is the creator of our creator?

❂

My grandfather spoke Yiddish. He refused to teach me. "Learn German, first. This isn't a ghetto." Yet it was; it was.

❂

O, the priceless pride of childhood.
I could move mountains then without realizing it…
I search through the broken pieces of the looking glass
trying to find my long-lost double.

❂

God talks to children, then makes them forget.
But sometimes, in dreams, we remember….

I wished on a falling star for a graceful falling

"Make a joyful noise unto the Lord!" That's what music is. All music, even the most despairing.

You can tell how close a man is to God by his acceptance; to the Devil – by his righteousness.

Opposites are conjoined twins, forever bound together.

◉

The Devil loves quoting prophets.

◉

Education and equality of women – the only chance for humanity to make it into the next century. As long as there is even one nine-year-old bride left – we all are doomed and deservedly so.

◉

Infinity is in each object,
just as God is within each person.
Infidels do not exist.

◎

You can believe or not believe. Just try to minimize hurting others.

◎

Time is a void, which needs art as its material. Without the arts, Time's monumental nonexistence would become too apparent.

◎

God was creative for six days. The rest of the time he was dealing with the consequences.

Negative emotions are often stronger than the positive, but the positive are more natural within the order of creation.

Leave revenge to the voodoo dolls.

Angels of daring, I call upon you!

◎

Lucky is the man who never meets his guru.

◎

Those who speak in the name of God are the Devil's favorite children.

◎

To know someone is to love him, is to accept him, is to accept yourself, is to love yourself, is to know yourself.

426 EXCESS OF BEING

Brainwashing is easy: Repeat the same words for 20 minutes five times a day. We are all programmable animals.

The seduction of religion is its certainty and the loftiness of its themes. Unfortunately, as with any literature, great subjects do not guarantee great execution.

Don't attach yourself to authoritative sources: Regardless of their reputation, they may be even more lost than you are.

❂

I'm adopting a new demon this week. He is an angel.

❂

The differences between beliefs are superficial. The moment we feel righteous or superior is the moment of loss, separation and confusion. We are all singing together, just different voices of the same fugue.

❂

Music is like loving, like living, like crying, like flying, like dying, like breathing; it possesses completely until everything becomes music: indivisible, inseparable, tender and violent in its oneness – until everything vibrates and sings with colors, until men know they are inseparable from God.

❍

Heritage is measured in losses.

❍

He is not reborn; he is rebranded.

❍

Space and Time exist only if you believe in them.

The Bible's translators were much more judgmental than its authors.

My blessings are taxable, but only by nostalgia.

Children are immortal until they learn the fairy tale of time.

Can you repeat who you are?
My reader?
Sorry,
I conjured you
by mistake!

My third eye knows best.

Forgetting comes easier than forgiving.

Light
blinds.
To see –
we turn away.
Our eyes hold
all images inverted.
Every day
a new Icarus
kills himself.

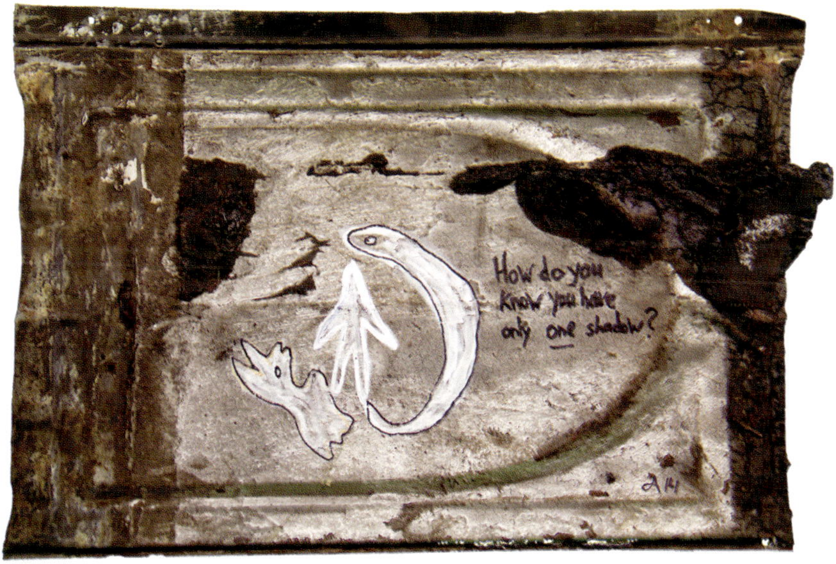
How do you
know you have
only one shadow?

Trouble Clef

Trouble Clef

88 Keys for Silent Piano:

1. Music: dreaming aloud.

2. Music notation: captured magic.

3. Music commissioner: investor in an intangible slice of immortality with his name on a score.

4. Chamber music: telepathy.

5. Composer: architect of silences.

6. Composer's work: lonely labor, indistinguishable from alchemy.

7. Compositional process: distilling passion into sounds.

8. Composer-in-residence: a living ghost.

9. Sounds: material of creation.

10. Conductor: (un)necessary evil.

11. Conductor: self-choreographer.

12. Conductor: fancy title for the orchestra's principal fundraiser.

13. Conducting: waving magic wand doesn't guarantee the magic.

14. Bad conductor: failed instrumentalist with an inflamed ego.

15. Good conductor: a necromancer, bringing the dead to life.

16. Orchestra manager: the guy who plays with his clock.

17. Musicologist: mortician.

18. Music presenter: someone who believes he has better artistic ideas than the artists he presents.

19. Theater curtain: an entity with a mind of its own.

20. Stagehands: big guys with headsets who prefer not to get their hands dirty.

21. Orchestra librarian: unacknowledged resident angel.

22. Dancers: butterflies.

23. Ballerina: choreographer's instrument.

24. Male dancer: ballerina's accessory.

25. Premiere: critic's alert to sharpen preconceptions.

26. Program notes: gravely misleading listening maps.

27. Microtonal notation: signal to play out of tune.

28. Phrasing: the search for gravity.

29. Intonation: tracing the holy ghost.

30. How to practice intonation? Mentally outline the ideal future and then make it reality.

31. Practicing: doesn't make anything perfect, but can create favorable conditions for accidental perfection.

32. Inspiration: The Muse doesn't forgive those who doubt her.

33. Technique: that which requires constant work to be unnoticeable.

34. Virtuosity: If you are complimented for it, you don't have it.

35. Tempo: (mostly) controlled flow of energy.

36. Meter: wagons in the train of Time.

37. Form: a map.

38. Unison: All is one.

39. Overtone series: proof of divine origins.

40. Fundamental tone: origins of the universe.

41. Accents: poking.

42. Expressions: desperate attempts of composer to communicate from beyond the grave, usually dismissed by performers.

43. Articulations: musicians' blind spots.

44. Pedal: misty and mysterious soul of the piano – routinely sterilized and castrated by pianists.

45. Repeat: that which never happens.

46. Repeat sign: *déjà vu*.

47. Last tremolo: preparation for standing ovation.

48. Rests: never restful.

49. Harmonic: sound's afterlife.

50. *Fermata*: the eye of time.

51. *Vibrato*: can cause nervous laughter.

52. *Dolce*: Tuck me in gently.

53. *Espressivo*: caffeinated emotions.

54. *Molto espressivo*: Make it double espresso.

55. *Morendo*: Did you hear anything?

56. *Pianissimo*: solo for the unwrapping of a candy.

57. *Pianississimo*: time for a hearing-aid's buzz.

58. *Caesura*: Breathe while you can.

59. *Glissando*: stretching space.

60. *Flautando*: memory of a sound.

61. *Sul ponticello:* the beast within, which you have repressed all your life.

62. *Con sordino*: taking the diva out of the violinist.

63. *Frullato*: growling in public.

64. *Staccato*: touching burning music with fingertips.

65. *Legato*: spilled slurs.

66. *Sforzando*: a musical ouch.

67. *Pizzicato*: pecking the grains of notes.

68. *Subito*: wife poking her husband when he starts to snore during a concert.

69. *Diminuendo*: magic mushroom in wonderland. You become smaller and smaller – as long as you are nibbling on it. Unfortunately, you never get small enough.

70. *Adagio*: Think of your mortality.

71. *Adagio molto*: Think of your immortality.

72. *Adagio religioso*: Pray for salvation.

73. *Allegro*: the original definition ('happily') no longer applies. Think general level of anxiety.

74. *Allegro molto*: think increased level of anxiety.

75. *Allegro con brio*: playing with fire.

76. *Andante*: The original definition ('leisurely walking') is extinct. Think depression.

77. *Moderato*: Comme ci, comme ça.

78. *Lento*: works better than Ambien for male audience members above the age of 50.

79. *Presto*: No thinking allowed.

80. *Vivace*: Act first. Regret later.

81. *Vivacissimo*: Jump off a cliff. You may or may not have time to open your wings.

82. *Stretto*: condensing time.

83. *Con moto*: You're running out of time.

84. *Accelerando*: seeing the light at the end of the tunnel.

85. *Ritenuto*: realizing what that light is.

86. *Ritardando*: Make every note count; you have very few of them left.

87. *Rubato*: loosening the reins.

88. *Ad libitum*: Create the illusion of freedom.

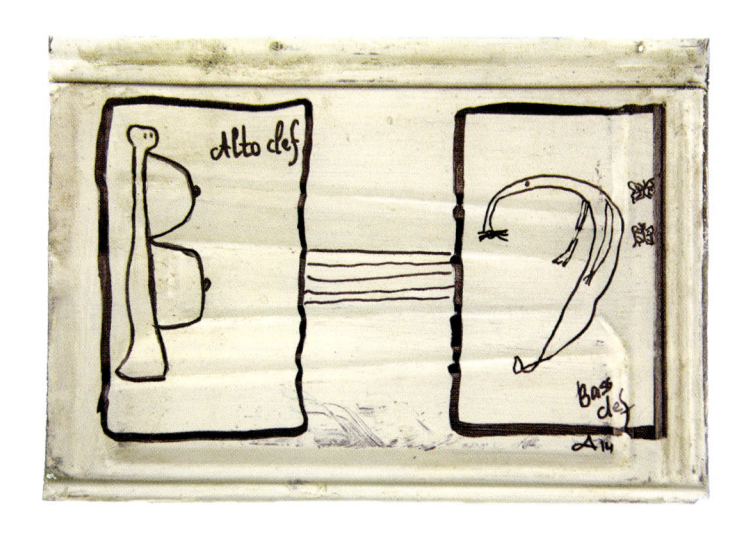

444 Excess of Being

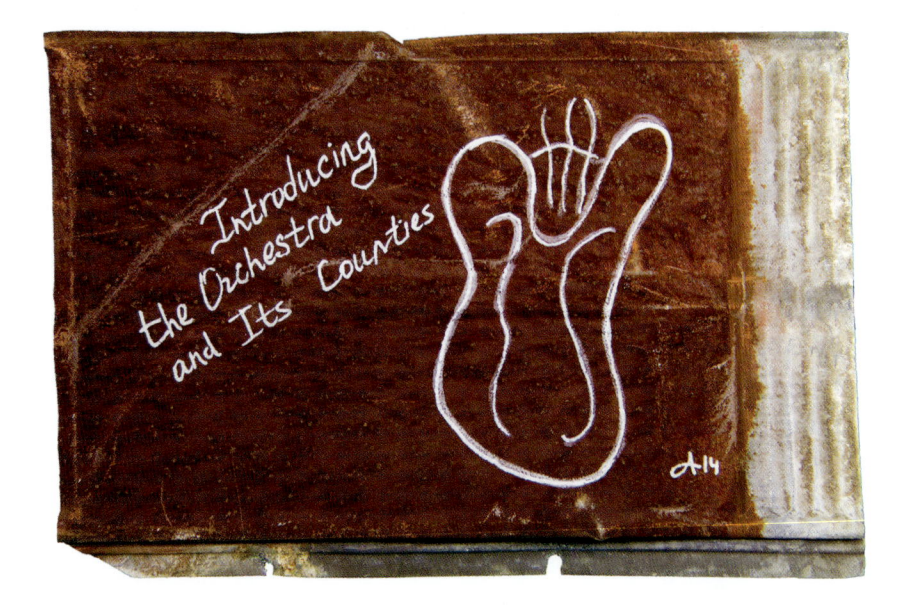

Introducing the Orchestra and Its Counties:

- Orchestra: democratic dictatorship.

- Piccolo flute: ears' toothpick.

- Piccolo's passages: scraping of the nervous system.

- Flute: skeleton of an exotic bird.

- Flute in the low register: unheard of.

- Alto flute: melted flute.

- Bass flute: imaginary friend that makes an occasional imaginary appearance.

- Block flute: a child's toy, requiring a highly specialized professional to perform.

- Oboe: permanently out-of-tune instrument, so much so that the rest of the orchestra has to tune to it.

- Oboist: a man who always tastes his instrument before playing it.

- First clarinet: exhibitionist of circular breathing.

- Bass clarinet: unfunny bassoon.

- Bassoon: royal jester.

- Contrabassoon: grandfather of the royal jester.

- Contrabassoon's staccato: old king's farts.

- French horns: cellos of the brass section with violinists' ambitions.

- Trombones: Throw a *glissando* at them and see what happens.

- Bass trombone: Mr. Macho Machissimo, married to Mrs. Tuba.

- Tuba: the golden halo of the orchestra.

- Mute for the tuba: Wouldn't you wish to have one for your spouse?

- Tuba's *frullato*: time for dinner.

- Orchestral pianist: percussionist who cannot count.

- Percussion section: the brains of the orchestra.

- Timpanist: arrogant percussionist.

- Harp: amplifier of silence.

- Harpist: harpy in disguise.

- Harp: undressed piano.

- Piano: a coffin for a harp.

- Piano: 88 keys for an unlocked door.

- Violin: prima donna.

- Cello: soul of the orchestra.

- Contrabass section: a mythological tortoise on which the world is built.

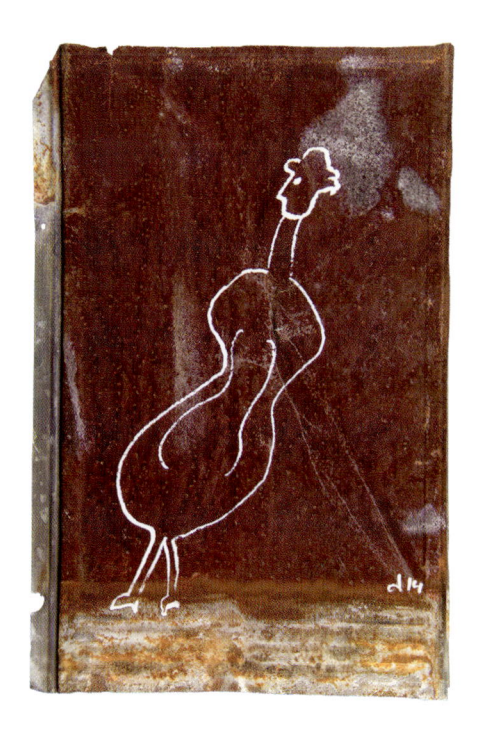

VOICES:

- Coloratura: female Icarus.

- Soprano: diva with an attitude.

- Mezzo-soprano: diva with a double attitude.

- Contralto: night butterfly.

- Countertenor: ghost of a castrato.

- Falsetto: baritone's alter ego.

- Tenor: self-centered lover.

- Baritone: fallen hero.

- Bass: hero with a belly.

- Boy soprano: an angel, already lamenting his inevitable fall.

- Chorus size: the more the merrier.

- Boys' choir: the more the naughtier.

- Vocal soloist: the (unholy) ghost during rehearsals, forever saving his voice for the glorious moment that will not arrive.

- Difference between an opera singer and a ballerina: At 30, the ballerina is overripe and her career starts rotting; at 30, the opera singer is not ripe enough and her career only starts flourishing. Unfortunately, one doesn't turn into the other.

Form and Content:

- Development à la Bach: premeditative execution.

- Development à la Beethoven: Disarticulate then put it back. Throw away parts that no longer fit and sprinkle with *sforzandi* to spice things up.

- Development à la Mozart: It's all about *il fila* – the breathing flow, the divine thread.

- Development à la Tchaikovsky: When out of ideas – repeat a step higher. If still out of ideas – repeat another step higher. It's called sequencing. Dancers love these things.

- Development à la Stravinsky: Take scissors, cut your score into small segments, mix them up and glue them back in a different order.

- Development à la Schoenberg: It's all about the journey, not the destination.

- Development à la Cage: Relax, give it all to chance.

- Development à la Boulez: absolute dictatorship – Boulez.

- Development à la Messiaen: Twitter away.

- Development à la Gesualdo: Put a child on a swing and sing him sweet madrigals until he dies.

- Development à la Debussy: Float away gently. Dream the colors.

- Development à la Glass: Write down three chords, then repeat them obsessively until your mind enters a hypnotic zone. Once in the zone, you need no development.

- Development à la Shostakovich: I've suffered enough. Now it's your turn.

- Development à la Rachmaninov: No keyboard is big enough for my fingers.

- Development à la Musorgsky: Throw an ax. Bleed randomly.

- Development à la Rimsky-Korsakov: Let's try to fit the Russian peasant into an elegant French suite. The result may be slightly bipolar.

- Development à la Bernstein: Love me; would you please love me? Would you please, please, please all love me *now*?

- Development à la Chopin: Let's condense all of life into a one-minute mazurka – to be played with bleeding fingers only.

- Development à la Liszt: I sold my soul to the Devil; that's why I pray to God.

- Development à la Schumann: It's all a private diary. Don't trespass on my soul.

- Development à la Penderecki: Burn it all down, then plant new trees.

- Development à la Crumb: There is no development. There is only experience of a given moment.

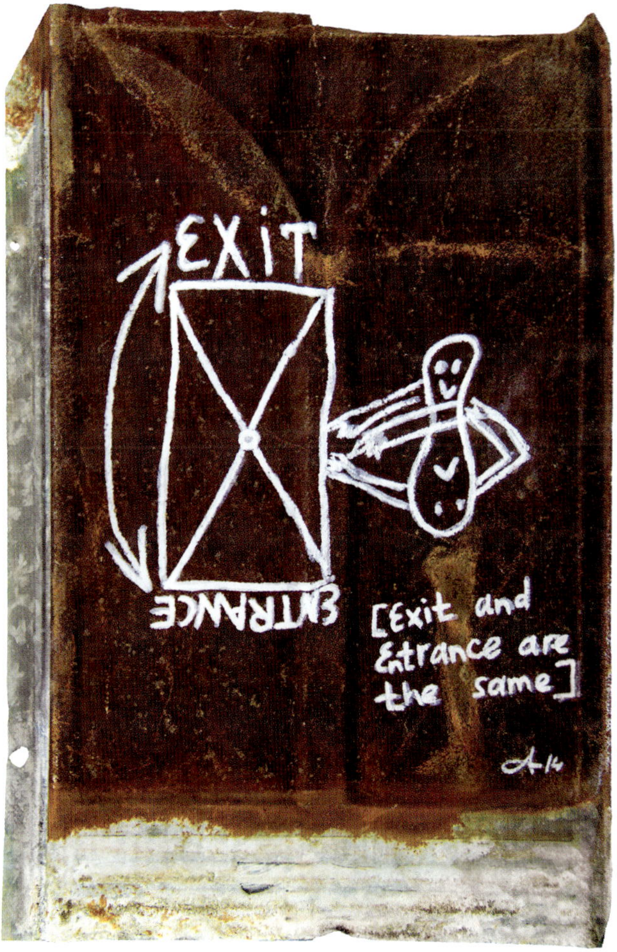
EXIT
ENTRANCE
[Exit and
Entrance are
the same]

Coda

Self-Portrait:

Wondering wanderer
in search of wonder,
always lost, never found,
profane and profound;
Circling sounds
through the maze of the page;
musical sage,
child of the times,
enchanted by rhymes,
seeking connection
in all forms of art,
forgetting her part
in everyday matters
(invoices, letters),
not knowing left from right,
hiding alone
in a secluded hut,
dying
from a paper cut.

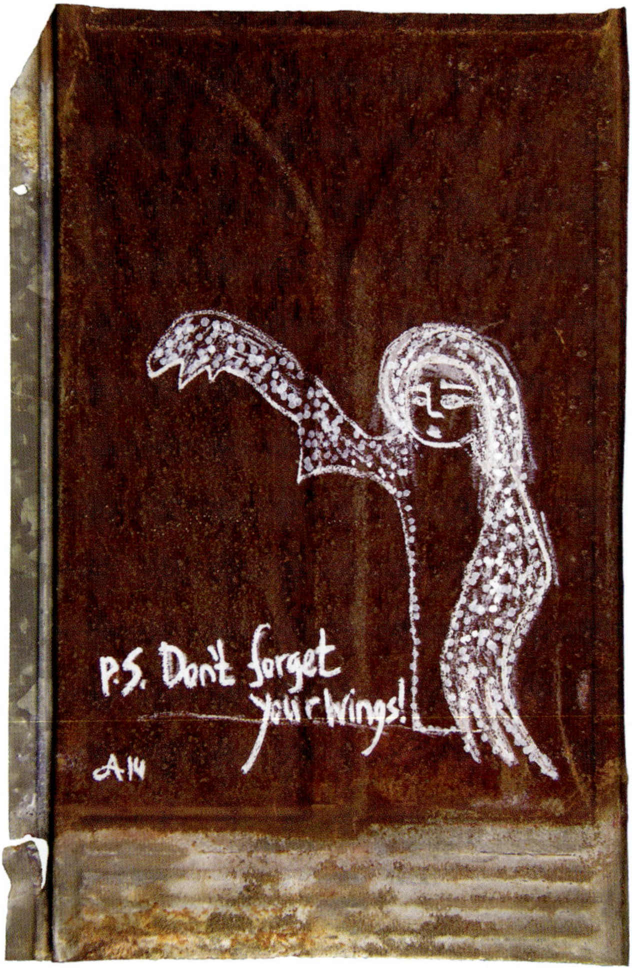
P.S. Don't forget
your wings!
A.14

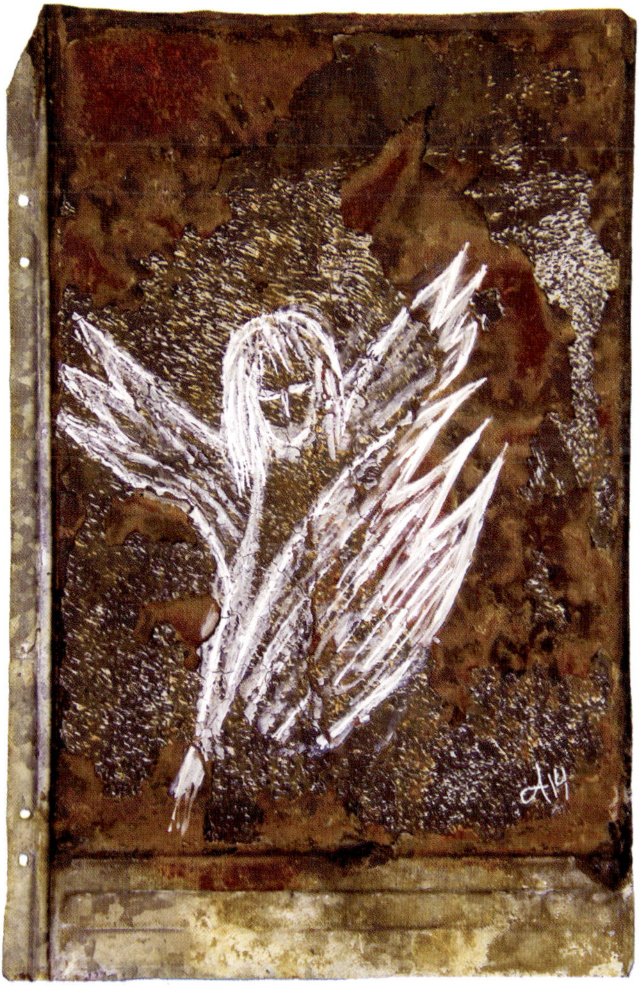

LERA AUERBACH, the Russian-American composer, writer, visual artist and concert pianist who performs regularly in major halls throughout the world, has published more than 120 works for orchestra, opera and ballet, as well as choral and chamber music. As pianist and composer, she graduated with bachelor's and master's degrees from the Juilliard School in New York and received her post-graduate degree as a concert pianist from the Hannover University of Music, Drama and Media in Germany.

Auerbach's works are performed internationally by the world's leading conductors, soloists, ensembles, choreographers and stage directors. She has been composer-in-residence with top orchestras and music festivals, including the Staatskapelle Dresden (Germany), São Paulo Symphony (Brazil), Verbier Festival (Switzerland), Trondheim Festival (Norway), Marlboro Festival (USA), MusikFest Bremen (Germany), Lockenhaus Festival (Austria) and Pacific Music Festival (Japan). CD and DVD releases of her works are available on the Deutsche Grammophon, ECM, ARTE, PBS, BIS, Capriccio and Cedille labels.

Auerbach is also prolific in literature and has published three books of poetry in Russian, which has been recited by major artists in performance. Her poetry and prose is included in various anthologies, as well as in the textbook of required reading for Russian high school literature classes. She is the author of several librettos and is a regular contributor to the Best American Poetry blog.

Auerbach often gives poetry readings (in Russian and English), presentations and talks, as well as master classes in various venues, including Harvard University, University of Michigan, Cleveland Institute, Open Society Institute in New York, Tokyo University, World Economic Forum in Davos, Switzerland, Music Center of

Budapest, Hungary, and the poetry festival of West Cork, Ireland, as well as festivals in Verbier, Aspen, Marlboro, Sapporo and others.

She has been drawing and sketching all her life as part of the creative process, and since 2009 has concentrated on painting and mixed media. Her art has been included in several exhibitions and, in 2013, she had her first solo exhibition in Norway. Her paintings are included in private collections, sold at auctions, reproduced in magazines, and used on the covers of CDs and books.

Auerbach's opera, *Gogol*, for which she wrote both the libretto and music, received its highly acclaimed world premiere in Vienna in 2011. Her groundbreaking a cappella opera, *The Blind*, has received productions in Germany, Norway, Russia, the United States and Austria. Her ballet, *The Little Mermaid*, was the winner of a 2012 ECHO Klassik award for Best Music DVD. It also received two Golden Mask awards and has been performed over 250 times worldwide. In 2014, on a commission by the Hamburg Ballet and the Stanislavsky Theater, she composed a two-act ballet, *Tatiana*, after Pushkin's *Evgeny Onegin*. She has also collaborated with, among others, the Netherlands Dance Theatre, Staatstheater Nürnberg, Munich State Ballet, Flanders National Ballet and Finnish National Ballet.

Auerbach has received numerous awards, including the prestigious Hindemith Prize, the Paul and Daisy Soros Fellowship, the German National Radio prize and the ECHO Klassik award, among others. The World Economic Forum selected Auerbach in 2007 as a Young Global Leader and in 2014 as a Cultural Leader, inviting her to give presentations and discussions on the fascinating topic of borderless creativity.

ART CATALOGUE 463

ROOFORISMS
by Lera Auerbach

OIL ON ANTIQUE METAL ROOF TILES

p. 14(I)  p. 17(IV)  p. 18(I)

p. 20(I)  p. 23(I)  p. 27(IV)

p. 29(I)  p. 31(I)  p. 32(6 x 14)  p. 34(I)

*All measurements in inches (I) 14 x 9.25 • (II) 9.25 x 14 • (III) 19 x 13 • (IV) 13 x 19

464 Excess of Being

p. 36(I)   p. 39(I)   p. 40(II)   p. 42(I)

p. 45(I)   p. 48(I)   p. 51(I)   p. 55(II)

p. 59(I)   p. 65(I)   p. 67(I)   p. 69(I)

p. 73(II)   p. 75(I)   p. 79(I)   p. 83(I)

Art Catalogue 465

p. 89(I)

p. 96(I)

p. 104(I)

p. 109(I)

p. 115(IV)

p. 124(II)

p. 133(I)

p. 139(I)

p. 145(I)

p. 147(I)

p. 149(I)

p. 152(I)

p. 157(I)

p. 162(I)

p. 167(I)

466 Excess of Being

p. 170(I)   p. 175(I)   p. 179(I)   p. 183(II)

p. 185(II)   p. 187(II)   p. 189(I)   p. 193(I)

p. 197(I)   p. 200(I)   p. 209(III)

p. 216(I)   p. 221(I)   p. 227(I)   p. 230(I)

ART CATALOGUE 467

p. 232(I)  p. 233(I) p. 236(II)  p. 245(I)

p. 250(I)  p. 254(I)  p. 259(I)  p. 263(I)

p. 267(III)  p. 269(I)  p. 271(I)

p. 274(I) p. 277(II)  p. 279(III)

468 Excess of Being

p. 288(I)   p. 294(I)   p. 300(I)   p. 306(I)

p. 311(I)   p. 316(I)   p. 321(I)   p. 328(I)

p. 333(I)   p. 335(II)   p. 341(IV)

p. 342(II)   p. 346(I)   p. 350(II)   p. 359(I)

ART CATALOGUE 469

p. 362(I)

p. 368(II)

p. 375(I)

p. 380(II)

p. 386(II)

p. 391(II)

p. 395(IV)

p. 404(II)

p. 409(II)

p. 414(II)

p. 420(II)

p. 426(II)

p. 431(IV)

p. 362(IV)

470 Excess of Being

p. 437(II) p. 443(II) p. 444(II) p. 447(I)

p. 4549(I) p. 433(I) p. 458(I) p. 459(I)

p. 475(I)

ART CATALOGUE 471

INK ON PAPER & MIXED MEDIA

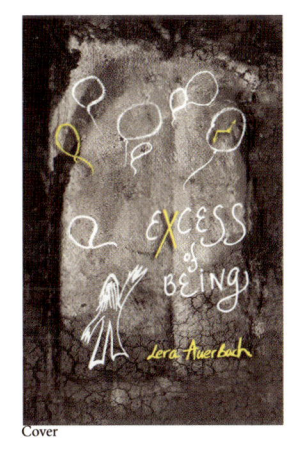

Cover

p. 11

p. 61

p. 141

p. 247

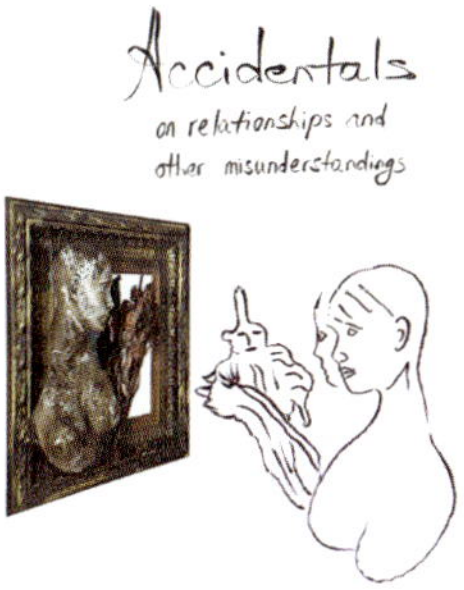

p. 281

p. 337

p. 435

p. 455

POSTLUDE

"A terrific read and a great companion, the kind of book that lovers of music and poetry will want to keep by their bedsides."
      Thomas McCarthy, poet, novelist and critic, author of *The Sorrow Garden* and *The Last Geraldine Officer*

"The real subject is your mind in motion – and your ear – and your nervous system… an inspiring experience."
      David Lehman, poet, editor for *The Best American Poetry* series, *The Oxford Book of American Poetry, Great American Prose Poems*, author of *A Fine Romance, Yeshiva Boys* and *The Evening Sun*

"One might think it enough for Lera Auerbach to be one of our best living composers and a virtuoso pianist. But she is also a poet and visual artist. This book of aphorisms, however, is a new departure. Books of aphorisms are pretty rare in our day, and even some very aphoristic poets–W.H. Auden comes to mind–never wrote one. Lera Auerbach's aphorisms are an open window on her mind, one of the best and busiest minds around just now."
      John Matthias, poet, editor of *Notre Dame Review*, author of *Different Kinds of Music* and *Collected Shorter Poems*

"Amusing and insightful, both fun and serious."
      Irene Dische, novelist, author of *Pious Secrets* and *The Empress of Weehawken*

"A great deal of wisdom and playfulness, and also a dark side that intimately reveals an inner world and beliefs: about everything from God, sex and music to literature."
    Josh Barkan, novelist, author of *Blind Speed* and *Before Hiroshima*

"Truly profound; made me think, wince and chuckle. Delicious reading."
    Antonina W. Bouis, award-winning translator, 'the best literary translator from Russian' according to *Publishers Weekly*. Her translations include *A Dog's Heart* by Mikhail Bulgakov, *Don't Die Before You're Dead* by Evgeny Evtushenko and *Shostakovich and Stalin* by Solomon Volkov

"*Excess of Being* is truly a very personal book, but it will make its readers think very deeply about their own situation in life, their existence and their visions. It is brilliant evidence of wisdom, life experience, humor and, above all, enjoyable reading."
    Hans-Ulrich Duffek, director and editor of Internationale Musikverlag Hans Sikorski, Hamburg

"Brilliant aphorisms. Gorgeous graphic art."
    Dmitry Gutov, visual artist

"From the world-renowned composer, visual artist and poet Lera Auerbach, *Excess of Being* at last affords us the opportunity to welcome a global talent to the anglophone stage."
    Taylor Davis-Van Atta, editor-in-chief of *Music & Literature*

What can be better than an aphorism? Its absence.